MANAGING BOYS' BEHAVIOUR

in your classroom

Greg Griffiths

Credits
Author: Greg Griffiths
Cover Design: Eva Ming Ling Kam
Book Design: Susana Siew-Demunck

Published in Australia by

HAWKER BROWNLOW
E D U C A T I O N

© 2002 Hawker Brownlow Education
PO Box 580
CHELTENHAM VIC 3192
Phone: (03) 9555 1344 Fax: (03) 9553 4538
Toll-free phone: 1800 334 603 Fax: 1800 150 445
Website: http://www.hbe.com.au
Email: brown@hbe.com.au

All rights reserved
Printed in Australia

Code #6697
ISBN 1 74025 669 7

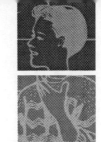

Contents

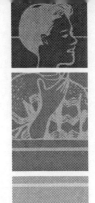

Foreword

'At last', teachers will say, 'a book about teaching boys that doesn't dwell on suicide rates or problematise dominant constructions of masculinity'. In recent years the support available to teachers has been heavily weighted at the theoretical, big picture end. Greg Griffith's practical emphasis in this publication is definitely needed. And his years of experience in assisting all manner of teachers, in all types of classrooms, shows through in his writing. His tone is respectful of teachers and the boys in their classrooms. He is not pointing out the 'right' way to teach or selling a brand new, revolutionary approach; in fact, many ideas will be recognisable as good teaching practice.

What Greg does offer are clear suggestions to improve boys' learning by paying attention to the basics, the environment and the rules, as well as ongoing issues of discipline, competition and relationships.

And his approach is based firmly on the ordinary teacher in an ordinary (that is, under-resourced) classroom.

Greg's teacher-based knowledge belongs in staffrooms around the country.

Lets hope that it is the first of many publications of this type, reflecting the recognition that teachers are key players in figuring out the nitty-gritty practice issues of educating future generations of men.

Richard Fletcher

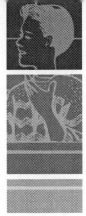

Introduction

There has been much written in recent years about boys in schools. As awareness of the varying success of boys and girls has increased, more research and material have become available. Boys' learning, boys' social interaction, boys' behaviour, boys not being involved in aspects of schooling, boys, boys, boys . . .

The following information has come to light:

- Boys are significantly more 'disengaged' with schooling and are more likely to be at 'risk' of academic achievement – especially in literacy.

- Boys exhibit significantly greater externalising behaviour problems in the classroom and at home.

- Fifty per cent of consultations to paediatricians at tertiary-referral hospitals relate to behaviour problems of boys to girls at a ratio of 9:1.

- Boys constitute 75–85 per cent of grade 1–2 children identified for Reading Recovery intervention.

- Boys have a higher prevalence of auditory processing problems.

- Boys report significantly less positive experiences in schooling in terms of enjoyment of school, curriculum usefulness and teacher responsiveness.

- Boys are more likely to 'drop out' prematurely. In 1994 to 1998 Australian national estimates indicate 30 per cent of boys did not complete their schooling, nor did 20 per cent of girls.

- Boys are subject to more disciplinary actions during school, are more likely to participate in delinquent behaviour, alcohol and substance abuse, and during adolescence are four to five times more likely than girls to suffer from depression and commit suicide.[1]

Why is this increasingly happening in recent years? There is evidence of a long-term decline in boys' performance, but no-one seems to have a satisfactory answer for the post-1990 performance difference, where girls have on average done better than boys and have improved on this year by year. Boys' performance has declined relative to girls'. The gender divide holds true in many circumstances: Aboriginal and Torres Strait Islander girls achieve better results in literacy tests than Aboriginal and Torres Strait Islander boys. It also seems that gender, class and race compound each other so girls from wealthier homes do better than working-class Anglo-Australian boys and some boys from ethnic groups.[2]

As the divide has become more apparent, debate and efforts to understand and rectify the discrepancy have been undertaken throughout the Western world. Unfortunately, we do not seem significantly closer to closing the gap between girls' and boys' academic performance nor the social divide. Consider the following:

- The male suicide rate is four times that of the female rate with the peak in the 15–24 year age group.

- When men and women are exposed to similar stressful events women show more anxiety-related depression; men show more substance abuse.

- Men aged 15–24 are between three and four times more likely to die from injury and over twice as likely to be hospitalised due to injury than young women.[3]

- Ninety-three per cent of the prison population is male with incarceration increase in recent years associated with violent crime.[4]

Education departments and schools have undertaken a variety of programs and alternative structures in an effort to address the issue of boys' achievement. They have had differing levels of success. In 1972 the US Department of Education passed a set of amendments aimed at reforming gender inequality in schools. This stated that 'no person . . . shall on the basis of sex be excluded from participation in, or denied the benefits of, or be subjected to discrimination, under any program or activity receiving federal aid'. However, the most well-known result was the encouragement and support of many girls' softball teams in public schools.[5]

It would seem that much of the effective work is being done at school level where schools identify issues relevant to their clientele and tailor programs to suit their conditions. This seems to be a major consideration in terms of a simple and all-embracing answer to the problem, which is perceived in many different forms. Through varying ages and cultural, geographic and educational settings, it is commonly recognised that boys are being outperformed, but the core problem contributing to this is not so universally agreed upon.

Five types of responses

While there has been a great variety of responses as schools identify different issues in different groups and cultures, the responses can be loosely grouped into five categories:

1. Disciplinary processes

Some schools have identified the issue as one where there are more boys than girls on detention, in the disciplinary processes, being suspended or being referred to behaviour services. These schools have tended to focus on discipline, with steps such as reviewing their disciplinary codes. In New South Wales there has been a concerted movement towards Choice Theory as a means of encouraging students to take responsibility for their own actions. With mainly boys undergoing disciplinary processes it would seem that discipline is an important issue, and while there have been some astounding successes, there have been some that have been less than successful. There are many reasons for the variation: speed of implementation, quality of implementation, clientele, support within the school and community and understanding of the processes being implemented.

A second factor here is the lack of resources in schools to positively influence students. Most schools have disciplinary policies and resources, but where many of these students are challenging school norms is in the gap between their home environments and/or socially accepted behaviours. Schools have resources to discipline students who have difficulty complying (we can tell them what not to do) but there do not appear to be the same resources available to positively demonstrate correct procedures (telling them what to do). This process is often seen in schools as being time- and resource-indulgent, and discipline codes are seen as more cost-effective methods of arriving at the desired short-term conclusion.

2. Knowledge-based approaches

Some schools have identified the issue as one of gender, and have questioned whether their students have sufficient knowledge of their own development and the issues this brings with it, as they are moving through their schools. These schools have addressed the issue through health- and physical education-type programs where gender construction and adolescence issues are raised and studied. There have been some outstanding successes, and some that have been less than successful. The variation might be explained through quality of implementation and longevity, relevance to the student body, mode of delivery and school setting issues.

3. Skill training

Some schools have identified that their boys may be lacking in conflict resolution skills, verbal articulation or general social skills. These schools have addressed the issue through social skills sessions, often as a 'one-off' or year-by-year session, such as through a Year 7 introductory camp or a Year 10–11 leadership group. There has been some reported success. However, without acknowledgment of the existence of these issues, monitoring and maintenance of the skills developed, school-wide acceptance of the issues, training for staff and students, and a culture where these skills are accepted and preferred, the longer-term success rate is questionable.

4. Individual personal development

Some schools have identified the particular individuals who have been causing the most concern. They have done this through looking at behaviour, academia and social interaction, and have developed programs to assist these students. These programs have often taken the form of 'Skill-streaming', 'Anger Taming', 'Talk Sense to Yourself', 'Stop, Think, Do' or many of the programs commercially available to address these skills within small groups. There has been some success, but these are very time- and resource-consuming programs. Schools have difficulty funding this sort of intervention for small groups for prolonged periods (and short interventions are not successful in the longer term).

5. Academic success

Some schools have identified academic success as a core issue. In recent years there has been a movement addressing boys' literacy and students with behaviour difficulties. Reading Recovery and myriad school-based learning and remediation programs have been run to improve reading levels of targeted students, often with considerable success. Whether this success transfers to other areas is yet to be fully assessed, and whether this addresses some of the issues for boys' behaviour is questionable. Some students could be 'acting out' when they are not experiencing success, but boys' behaviours such as risk-taking, testing the rules and not wanting to be seen as successful – if that means breaking from the group – are not being catered for and continue to cause concern.

While schools have been trying methods to address a variety of issues throughout the whole school, research published in 1999 by Peter West[6] in a project questioning the relative value of sport compared to schooling and what sport was teaching boys about 'being a man' suggests some conclusions that are important for classroom teachers. His survey of students across four schools in Sydney, while focusing on masculinity, suggests the following:

- Much more research needs to be done on school culture. Changing the culture of masculinity in the school may open up some possibilities for changing boys' behaviour and performance.

- One of the key factors in UK research is the attitude of the teacher. (This also parallels the research by Dr Ken Rowe at ACER.)

- Teachers must stay flexible to channel boys' energetic and exuberant masculinity. Some argue that computers are an important part in staying abreast of boys' mental development, yet with ageing teachers and poor resources many schools are falling behind (with the probable exception of some wealthy schools). Socialisation is increasingly being over shadowed by TV, videos and the Internet while schools as a socialising agent are becoming increasingly irrelevant. (Compare this with research at Flinders University, page 33.)

- Boys respond to people who listen to them.

- Many of us have ingrained attitudes about boys and girls. We may be forcing attitudes on boys which are no longer appropriate.

- We need more research on who is getting the rewards in schools. When sporting awards and presentations at school assemblies outweigh academic awards or recognition of social activity, the balance, in boys' minds, may tip to one side.

- The power of sport to move boys to great emotional heights and depths needs careful investigation. Boys in this study showed strong feelings about sport and sportsmen. Reports from the Columbine High School massacre suggest that certain boys resented 'the jocks' and the violent rampage there was in part because of this resentment.

- UK schools are specifically required to comment separately on boys' and girls' performance. UK schools have found that the quickest way to improve school performance is to address boys' underachievement. Specifically requiring schools to report on boys' performance ensures this issue is paid more than just lip-service.

While this research has been aimed at masculinity issues, these conclusions seem relevant for all our classrooms and have something to offer teachers who face the daily grind of motivating and stimulating their classes.

This short book is not aiming to address the larger issues that may involve whole-school communities, if not systems, reviewing their practice in light of boys' performances. It focuses on the classroom practitioner and classroom management – especially for boys. There is no preference for a system of welfare management nor particular disciplinary systems or processes. There will not be debate about middle schools or single-sex classes or schools. Schools utilise many different methods, and for many their success is determined by how they are locally responsive rather than the veracity of their overarching philosophy.

This book includes steps for classroom management that classroom teachers can employ in most school environments to assist learning for both boys and girls.

Preparation of meaningful, relevant, interesting lessons is left to the undoubted skill and expertise of the classroom teacher supported by the curriculum. There will not be comment on literacy or numeracy issues, the relevance of particular curriculums will not be examined, nor will school management, and gender issues within school administration will not raise its head. Community concerns about suicide, risk-taking and drug use will not be addressed. And the broad issue of masculinity, while certainly recognised, will remain a backdrop. This book is about classroom management, especially for boys.

Kindergarten to senior secondary school teaching, in co-ed schools, generally involves interacting with groups of students, about half of whom will be male. Unfortunately, the track record of these boys is not good. They seem to take more teacher time than girls, more discipline time, are more often found in detention rooms, remedial classes, corridors, principals' offices and special classes.

From kindergarten to Year 12. What can we do?

Here are a series of techniques and procedures that may make classroom life a little easier. Some are relevant to primary and infants classrooms, some are more pertinent to secondary groups, but most can be adapted for either, with a little imagination.

There are few resources required here other than teacher time and energy (one of the most precious resources we have in schools). Nothing here will disadvantage girls. Effective classroom management in itself will benefit all students and the practices outlined here can involve girls just as well as boys. However, boys' actions are attracting so much teacher attention that a focus on good classroom practice towards the boys could improve learning outcomes for all students.

Following is a short list of behaviours exhibited by boys and girls that, although not directly associated with their learning, will have an impact in the classroom. Teachers will identify these and many others that differentiate boys' and girls' classroom performances. These are the sorts of behaviours that this book attempts to address. It is not meant to be philosophical but practical, with processes that are within the scope of classroom teachers to improve the outcomes for boys and girls in their classes.

Throughout this book reference will be made to 'boys preferring . . .' or 'boys are good at . . .', and it should be understood that these are generalisations made from experience and research. Some boys will not fit stereotypical images, and some boys would not fit the characteristics noted below. Some boys do very well in our schools and find the learning environment suitable, but a quick review of Rowe's data demonstrates that, en masse, there are aspects of schooling that are not enticing or attractive to boys.

At the end of each year there is debate over elite results. In recent years media reports suggest girls have the edge. But many boys are also in this elite group and while generalisations are made about boys' performance being below that of girls, we should note that some boys are succeeding at the elite level and some will continue to do so in the future.

Similarly, some boys complete their schooling without confronting school discipline codes or behaviour management programs at anything but the least intrusive level. However, the suspension and discipline records of schools show that as a group boys

Girls tend to	Boys tend to
• move quietly in corridors	• move physically and loudly in corridors
• bring equipment	• not have equipment
• complete homework	• not complete homework
• focus on quality work	• focus on completing tasks
• ask fewer questions	• want to ask questions
• ask questions appropriately	• want immediate response
• watch during practical sessions	• dominate during practical sessions
• not participate when not engaged	• disrupt when not engaged
• discuss work	• work alone
• discuss personal issues	• discuss sport or movies
• cooperate with others	• compete with others
• comply more readily	• test instruction
• be able to ignore disruption	• move off task more easily
• accept redirection	• confront redirection

receive greater attention than girls.

Comments on boys' behaviour in this book do not refer to *all* boys. Rather, these comments reflect characteristics that academic research, anecdotes, classroom experience, staffroom scuttlebutt, literature and a few years as a parent have identified as being gender-related but not exclusively or conclusively *male*.

Preparation

One of the great stresses is the unknown. Every time we walk into a classroom there are individuals who are influenced by factors that we have little knowledge about and even less chance of changing. While we may have limited opportunities to alter these influencing factors, we can try to influence the students and we can most certainly be sure of our own processes within the school. If teachers are unsure about school or classroom processes, this uncertainty will be explored by the students.

Boys are the barometer. They will challenge rules and processes until the limits are determined and all are aware of them. Even then there will be sporadic forays just to check that the parameters haven't been changed while no-one was looking. If teachers demonstrate variation, lack of certainty or willingness to be swayed, and boys will try to manipulate this for their own benefit.

All teachers have heard 'Miss Smith lets us do that' or 'We don't have to do this with Mr Brown' as students resist an instruction, try to find a crack or convince the instructor that they really should not have to do something. Discrepancies from one classroom to the next will always occur – teachers are human – but each of us can reduce the inconsistencies within our own domain.

Careful planning of the content of each lesson consumes a great deal of teacher preparation time and the same energy needs to be channelled into management. All too often in staffroom and community discussions behaviour of students, and the way this behaviour is changing, is the key topic. Many teachers suggest a significant part of their class time is spent on discipline rather than teaching, and as problems with student behaviour escalates, teachers are left wondering what tools they have remaining with which to manage.

Planning and preparation for behaviour management can only assist teachers when intervention is needed. Ensuring school policy and procedures are known by all staff members and that policies are regularly reviewed to retain freshness, relevance and ownership can remove that feeling of uncertainty sometimes experienced when student behaviour becomes unacceptable. Regular review of school policy also promotes consistency among staff. At grade, faculty, stage or cohort level, regular review of classroom practices and discussion with buddy teachers and colleagues 'at the chalkface' keeps practitioners conversant with emerging behaviours and development of management tools.

Preparation for behaviour management within school policies involves the following:

- understanding and accepting the rights of students and staff
- understanding the responsibilities for all parties which support these rights
- negotiating and maintaining fair rules with known and logical consequences
- establishing positive relationships with students
- developing routines that encourage student confidence

The following diagram illustrates these points.

Figure 1   What the school community believes are the core values of the school

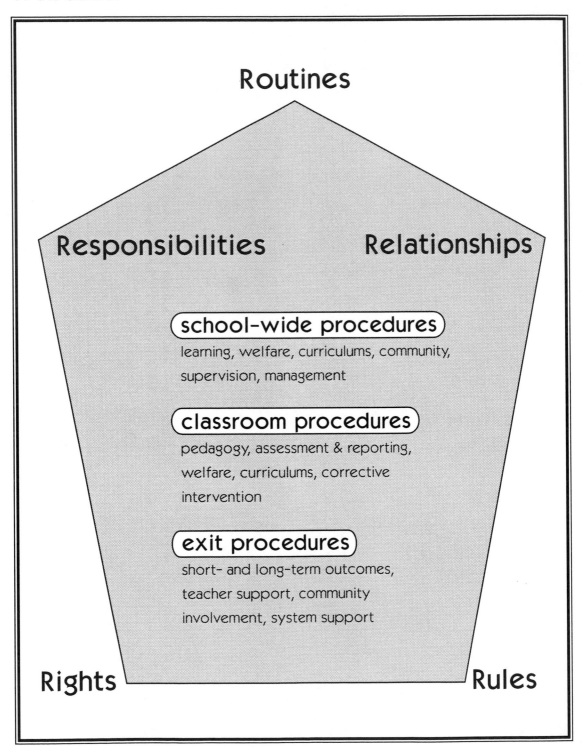

Routines

Responsibilities   **Relationships**

school-wide procedures

learning, welfare, curriculums, community, supervision, management

classroom procedures

pedagogy, assessment & reporting, welfare, curriculums, corrective intervention

exit procedures

short- and long-term outcomes, teacher support, community involvement, system support

Rights   **Rules**

This book is based on the following basic premises for successful classroom management. All students and teachers have rights and responsibilities. The rules, relationships and routines that we develop support these in our classrooms.

The 5 Rs

Rules

Rights

Routines

Relationships

Responsibilities

Each of these '5 Rs' will be reviewed in the context of working with boys, suggesting practices that will assist in their management, but which will also create a positive learning environment for all students. With each section is a short list of considerations, strategies, guides or prompts that may prove useful.

Teaching staff should prepare mentally for the behaviours that are being presented and practise management techniques so that, when an event does occur in their classroom, they can feel relatively experienced and present a facade of control and certainty. Having prepared for events, when they do occur, teachers can be **sure** of their reactions, **sure** that school policy is carried out and **sure** that their procedures comply with best practice.

These 5 Rs apply equally to the most extreme behaviour and to behaviour that requires much less intrusive intervention (see Figure 1).

Notes

1. K. Rowe, 'Exploding the "myths" and exploring "real" effects in the education of boys', *The boys in schools bulletin*, University of Newcastle, Queensland, vol. 3, no. 3, 2000.

2. P. West, 'Boys' underachievement in school: some persistent problems and some current research', *Issues in educational research*, vol. 9, no. 1, 1999.

3. UHCMI & University of Newcastle, *Rural young men's health report*, Newcastle, 2000.

4. Australian Institute of Criminology, Australian Crime: facts and figures, Canberra, 2000

5. GREAT, vol. 1, issue 1, 1998.

6. ibid.

Figure 2   The Five Rs

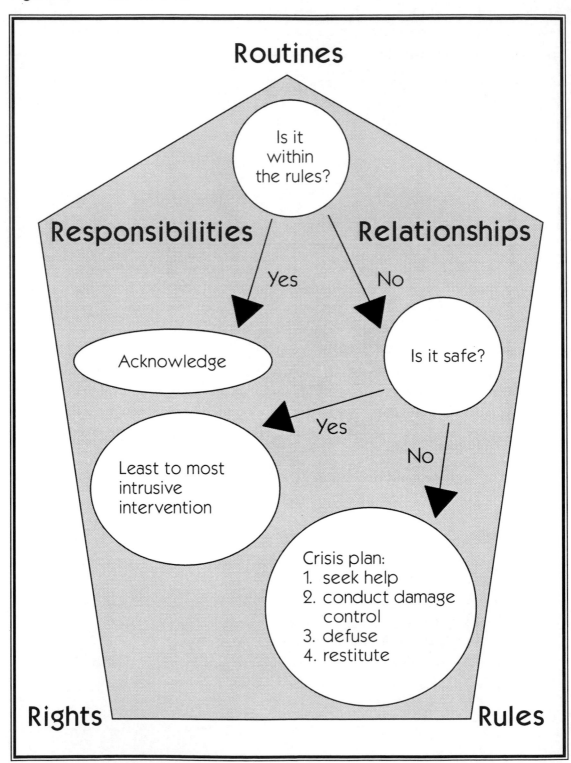

part 1

Foundations

The physical environment

The general factors of the physical environment include the following:

- Layout of classroom, which includes
  - size of group
  - space available
  - furniture
  - carpet – noise and cleaniness
  - desks – mobility and arrangement
- School tone, which includes
  - general climate – firm, clear
  - size of school
  - expectations
  - limits on behaviour
  - tolerance of behaviour
  - acceptance of students
- Classroom tone, which includes
  - acceptance of student but not the behaviour
  - warmth
  - awareness and sensitivity
  - flexibility
- Interpersonal skills and staff morale, which include
  - cooperation
  - trust and honesty
  - emotional maturity
  - sharing of burdens
  - relieving of feelings
  - absence of fear of reprisal

Before students enter the classroom, teachers taking a look at the physical environment could assist their time here. Just as we prepare curriculum content, learning experiences and behaviour management, a small amount of time could be well spent preparing the room. Even before considering the class itself, some future situations may be relieved by a review of distractions in the room, teacher desk location, seating arrangements, and student flow in and out of the room. Many classrooms are works of art, with students' work displayed at every corner, and stimulus material for current topics at students' fingertips. These are colourful, inviting rooms. Whether it be the student, teacher, parent or community member entering the room, it provides a welcoming experience. Primary and infants' rooms are most often in this group.

Some classrooms, particularly ones in which teachers and students move about each lesson, are not so inviting. Often these rooms are devoid of much stimulus and student work is often not displayed. Secondary classrooms too often fall into this group. Rational and understandable reasons are put forth for not displaying students' work, stimulus material and not taking the time to make the rooms more attractive. These reasons include vandalism, an inability to monitor classes using the room, theft and lack of respect for the students' work and teacher material being displayed. Teachers who have made an effort and experienced these issues often have personal stories to tell that do not encourage improving a classroom's appearance. But teachers who have succeeded have as many stories of greater student interest and participation.

Often underlying these discussions are school structures and whether staff or classes have home rooms and whether they are mobile. Primary teachers most often are more sedentary than their secondary colleagues (some specialist secondary teaching areas have home rooms, e.g. science) and this has an impact, as does the age of their students.

The bottom line for encouraging student attention and interest is an inviting room. Education literature is filled with examples of teachers who when faced with 'the class from hell' on Friday (or any other afternoon), proactively took the initiative and created interesting environments which overcame the behaviour of classes reputed to incur early teacher retirement. Looking only within the classroom, whether the teacher or class is mobile or not, a more inviting classroom can only assist in encouraging students to learn.

While making the room enticing for students is a first step, it is just that. Boys in particular will lose interest in stimulus that does not change. Wonderful maps, pictures, classwork or other material that remains on display too long ceases to be seen let alone appreciated. Constantly changing material encourages investigation, and boys will investigate. They will want to see how something works, what that poster is about, what this set up is, etc. When they have discovered the how, what, when and why, their interest quickly falls away. Then it's time for a change. It might be that relocation is sufficient, but regular change is necessary to keep students' – especially boys' – interest alive.

Some classrooms have a 'wall of excellence' where students' work is displayed for a short period. As new work of good quality is completed – and with the student's

permission – it is displayed for the class. This keeps the work and stimulus changing, reinforces for all students that quality work is sought, demonstrates what quality work is and gives reinforcement to students. For the boys, it shows the following:

- perfect work is not always required

- their work is valued

- others are achieving at about their level and are being appreciated

- that an effort to achieve is recognised

- what others are doing so that they can pick up hints without being demeaned or embarrassed in class

Constant change is necessary to entice interest in and investigation of the material.

Time should also be spent determining where the distractions in the room are, what distractors are outside the room, checking the seating arrangements and flow of traffic to obtain the best situation before students arrive.

Once boys are distracted from their classwork, the task of encouraging them back can be a little difficult. While girls will more readily return to work after a minimal distraction, for many boys there is no turning back. Once their attention has shifted from their work, new stimuli are sought, usually with others. Sitting easily distracted boys where they have full view of class computer screens, on a main traffic way within the class, beside the classroom door, or in any position where there are more distractions than elsewhere in the room, may be courting disruption that a little preparation might reduce. If the environment is reviewed, some of the ensuing difficulties that we are all familiar with may not arise.

Seating arrangements can also have an effect on class tone. Consider the following points:

- Long rows of desks with access at either end make it difficult for the teacher to assist students in the centre, create bag problems and traffic funnels. Conversely, this arrangement has every student facing the front and reduces the number of students seated on aisles. Boys who generally prefer to sit at the back and sides of the class are in the most accessible places in this arrangement.

- Groups of two or three desks in parallel rows reduces the bag-behind-the-row problem, increases the number of students on an aisle, reduces traffic funnels and increases peer group formation. This arrangement allows teachers access to different students and an opportunity to be out of eyesight of students on task.

- Desks in scattered groups can further reduce traffic problems, may reduce the number of students facing the front, may increase the number of students facing each other and may allow students to develop varying peer groups. Teacher access

is good, though the opportunity to be out of sight is reduced.

- Allowing students to sit wherever they wish allows flexibility of peer group movement, can increase dissent over particular arrangements, may allow exclusion of individuals by groups and can have an impact on group work.

The list of variations is much longer than this short group, and the arguments for and against various seating arrangements are even longer. Rather than determine a single pattern, class dynamics and the lesson type might impact on the optimal arrangement. However, frequent alterations can have negative effects, too, by breaking routines established within the class, and, depending on the frequency with which you occupy the room, can cause disquiet with other staff members if seating arrangements are regularly changed.

Many boys view changed seating patterns as an opportunity to test the following:

- where they can sit
- who they can sit with
- if class rules still apply
- whether the seating pattern is 'better' than its predecessor
- if they can re-establish their position in the class order

Change is often an opportunity for further change. If there is value in altering class seating arrangements, this should be done keeping in mind that there could also be behaviour implications.

The classroom environment

Does the classroom layout

- · best suit the size of the group?
- · best use the space available?
- · best use the furniture available?
- · allow mobility or variation for alternate groups?
- · create corridors or funnels?

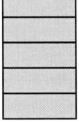

Does the placement of the teacher's desk

- · dominate the room?
- · anchor the teacher to one spot?
- · focus attention?

Does the classroom

- · invite students to enter and learn?
- · display students' work?
- · have learning material on display?
- · show interaction between student and teacher?
- · visually display classroom rules?

cont.

For the present layout, consider the

ADVANTAGES	DISADVANTAGES

What are some changes that would assist management?

Draw your current layout.

Make a list of physical distractions.	What can be done about these?

On the map of your room, mark in red any physical distractors you have identified.

Make a note of other distractions particular to the room.

Is there something you can do about these other distractions?

Complete the room map by allocating seats to your students and colouring those students you recognise as having significant learning or behaviour difficulties in blue.

Compare your map with that of a 'buddy' teacher and discuss your plan with them.

cont.

Do		
• all students seat themselves where they wish?	YES	NO
• some students seat themselves where they wish?	YES	NO
• some students sit where the teacher indicates they sit?	YES	NO
• disruptive students sit where they wish?	YES	NO
• disruptive students sit where they distract other students?	YES	NO
• students with reduced attention spans sit near distractions?	YES	NO
• you place students with reduced attention spans near distractions?	YES	NO
• you think this is the best arrangement for classroom management?	YES	NO
• you think these seating changes improve classroom management?	YES	NO

What problems can be foreseen?	What can be done in preparation for these?

If there are changes to make, map them below.

Figure 1.1   Rights

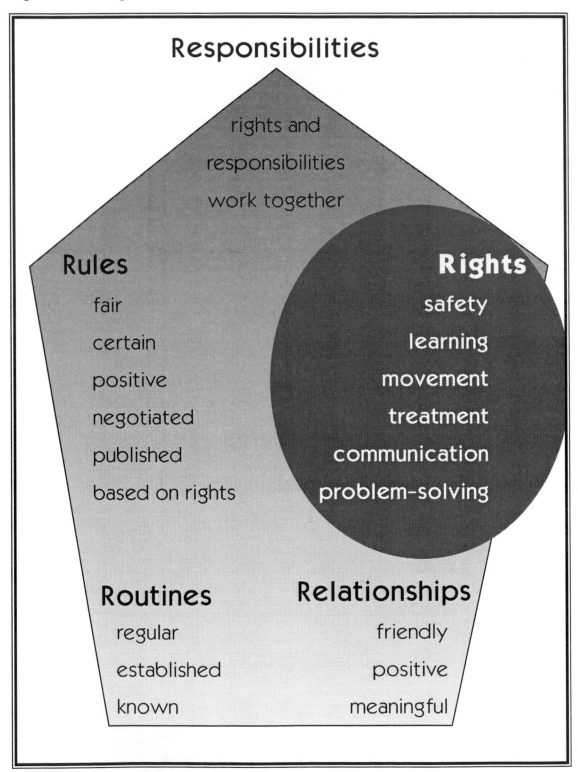

Responsibilities

rights and
responsibilities
work together

Rules

fair

certain

positive

negotiated

published

based on rights

Rights

safety

learning

movement

treatment

communication

problem-solving

Routines

regular

established

known

Relationships

friendly

positive

meaningful

Rights

We all have rights. Male or female, young or old, migrant, indigenous, ethnic minority or majority. The United Nations as well as many other countries have determined the bill of rights for individuals. Without formally establishing such a document, students in our schools also have rights. Consider the following list:

Possible rights of students

I have the right to be happy and to be treated with understanding

I have the right to be treated with respect and politeness

I have the right to express my opinion on matters of concern to me

I have the right to be safe

I have the right to be helped to learn self-control

I have the right to expect my property to be safe

I have the right to obtain maximum benefit from all classes

I have the right to have a pleasant, clean and well-maintained school and grounds

I have the right to expect the local community to support, respect and have pride in the school

I have the right to not be ignored if others abuse my rights

I have the right to expect that all these rights will be mine so long as I am carrying out my full responsibilities

Bill Rogers[1] has established a more succinct set of rights for students. He states:

> It is important to focus on the essential rights from which all others spring. These rights are non-negotiable. They are not merely culturally based or gender based. Everyone has the right:

- To feel safe at school. Students cannot learn well or socialise effectively if they feel unsafe in classrooms or playgrounds. Emotional and physical safety, therefore, are high priorities in student management.

- To learn to the best of their ability with the best of assistance

- To be treated with dignity and respect – even when they are being disciplined.

Further rights are suggested as flowing from these 'core' rights. They are:

- Communication – students should be able to expect others to speak kindly and respectfully to them.

- Movement – this should be possible, safe and non-disruptive around the school and classroom.

- Problem-solving – this should be conducted in a fair manner. It should apply to all

students and be widely accepted. The rights of students are not variable by gender, and these simple rights should form a solid basis.

Some rights that are accepted within society may be curtailed in schools, but students also enjoy 'trade-off' benefits. For example, some schools place restrictions on students travelling in cars driven by their peers. Society generally does not prevent individuals travelling with their friends and acquaintances but schools often restrict this right. For those students wishing to ride home with a mate after a day's lessons, this may be hard to understand, but there are implications for schools. Conversely, there are often reports of school students appearing in juvenile courts as a result of their actions, where the magistrate has suspended or quashed a conviction on the condition that the student returns to school.

The structures within our schools are essentially there to protect and enforce the rights of individuals and groups. In recent years students have become more aware of their rights and have been asserting them increasingly. This has presented some difficulties in classrooms and schools where youthful zeal may not also register that along with personal rights come personal responsibilities, thus allowing others their rights as well. The manner in which rights are asserted and/or defended in the playground or classroom can often miss the subtleties of debate in the Old Bailey.

Whether the student be male or female, rights are inalienable. On occasion many students' actions infringe on the rights of others as they learn to navigate the nuances of society, learn what they can and cannot do, learn what is expected of them as they grow and develop and start realising that their actions have an impact on others. Their responsibilities may need to be revisited to ensure the smooth functioning of the school community.

Adolescent boys in particular seem prone to focus inwardly and often the rights of others are trampled in their innocent endeavours to assert and understand themselves. Revisiting their responsibilities without removing their rights can take on another dimension if frustration and anger surface in the process.

While the manner in which students use and defend their rights may vary in time and place, the maintenance of their rights is at the very core of student welfare within our schools.

There should also be recognition of the rights of staff. Over many years workers in all areas of employment have increasingly sought safe workplaces, and teachers are not an exception.

> ## Possible rights of teachers
>
> *I have the right to teach in a climate that is free from disruption*
>
> *I have the right to expect behaviour from students which contributes to their optimal growth*
>
> *I have the right to limit students' inappropriate, self-destructive behaviour*
>
> *I have the right to ask for, and receive help and backing from, administrators and parents*

In mid-2001 the National Education Association – the largest teacher union in United States – offered its members an 'unlawful homicide' benefit for the family members of any person killed at work. Over a nine-year period, twenty-nine US teachers died violently at school.[2] While this is the extreme, our society is becoming increasingly violent and this is reflected in our classrooms.

In New South Wales, from 1999 to 2000, suspensions for students who have not been able to comply with school policies have increased by 15 per cent (with about 5 per cent of students suspended at least once during the year[3]), with a further increase in 2001 ('School violence', *The Sydney Morning Herald*, 23 December 2001). It has been reported that, after two annual increases of over 20 per cent, Education Queensland shut down its database of suspensions.[4] These increases in suspensions demonstrate students are increasingly questioning barriers and finding difficulty accepting the limitations to their actions imposed by schools. However, the rules that schools establish are in place to protect all students' rights and those of the staff. When there are increasing rates of rules being seriously transgressed, it could be appropriate to review the rights of all stakeholders.

At the extreme of the school rules there may be a blending of school discipline and societal law enforcement, where the rights of students or staff are transgressed not just in terms of the school rules but also as individual members of a greater society.

Teachers may not be the target of actions leading to suspension and for many teaching staff their interactions with students are entirely pleasant and supportive, but some staff face angry and often violent youth trying to establish their own boundaries and searching for the tools with which to succeed. The following news stories illustrate this.[5]

Schools of violence

The Sunday Telegraph, 19 August 2001

Teachers forced to take out AVOs against pupils

BY KATRINA CREER

TEACHERS have taken out almost 200 apprehended violence orders against students, parents and other staff members in government schools.

The AVOs were prompted by a range of serious incidents, including one where a student spiked his teacher's drink with methylated spirits, an investigation by *The Sunday Telegraph* has revealed.

The Department of Education says more students than ever before are being suspended for violent acts.

In NSW last year, 16,972 students were suspended from government schools for violence, an increase of 11 per cent from 1999. Another 2690 students were given longer suspensions for more serious acts of violence, a rise of 17 per cent.

Freedom of Information documents obtained by *The Sunday Telegraph* show 102 AVOs have been taken out by teachers against students and ex-students in the past four and a half years.

Another 55 have been sought against parents, 22 against members of the community and five against other staff members.

Line of fire

- Teachers have sought 102 apprehended violence orders against students or ex-students from 1997 to June.

- 55 were sought against parents.

- 22 were taken out against members of the community.

- Five were sought against other members of staff.

Former science teacher ███████, who sought an AVO after he was punched in the face by a student, believes the real figure could be much higher because teachers are too scared to report violence.

'I didn't want anyone to know I couldn't cope,' he said. 'You feel a loss of your sense of worth and dignity.'

Mr Parson was working at ████ High School in 1997 when he was assaulted by a Year 8 student in 1997 seeking revenge

after being transferred to another school because of disruptive behaviour.

'I didn't even see him – the first thing I knew I was smacked in the mouth and then kneed in the groin,' ████████ said.

████████ sought an AVO because he was afraid the boy would harass him at home.

Six months later, another student screamed obscenities at him in a classroom.

████████ eventually left teaching.

A home economics teacher, who did not want her name published, said she was too frightened to seek an AVO after being verbally abused by a parent.

Bev Baker, of the Parents' and Citizens' Association, said schools are overzealous in suspending students for behaviour such as threatening language.

Teachers who take out AVOs against children deny them of an education, she warned.

Boy suspended over toy gun

The Daily Telegraph, 3 July 2001

A 15-year-old student who pointed a toy gun at a teacher's head and pulled the trigger several times is to be recommended for youth conferencing.

The youth is currently serving the maximum 20-day suspension from ████ High School following the incident which occurred last Tuesday.

The female teacher involved was reported to have been badly shaken by the incident which took place in a Year 9 English class. She has taken time off and is receiving counselling.

Police have carried out a full investigation into the incident.

A spokesman said yesterday the matter was referred to a specialist youth liaison officer who has recommended the student be conferenced.

He has also been offered counselling through the Department of Education.

Twenty days is the maximum period of suspension under procedures introduced by the Department of Education in 1999.

Historically, boys make up about 75–80 per cent of suspensions and, when this is accompanied by Bureau of Statistics research indicating boys are spending less time on 'educational activities'[6], the achievement of satisfactory outcomes for some in this group becomes jeopardised.

Many would raise the issue that society itself is becoming more violent, and that these figures mirror trends outside our schools. They may have a point. Australia has witnessed an increase in imprisonment rates from 1983 to 1999 of four per cent annually. This increase appears to be largely due to the increase in prisoners being sentenced for violent offences. While the number of prisoners sentenced for these types of offences has more than doubled between 1983 and 1999, the population aged 17 years and over increased by only 30 per cent. Just over 6 per cent of all prisoners in 1999 were women.[7]

Apart from these incarceration figures, the media is full of 'rage'.[8] If these trends are reflected in our schools, then revisiting individuals' rights, including those of the teaching staff, is not too far out in left field.

| Angry city | The Daily Telegraph, 3 July 2001 |

What gets us really worked up

ROAD RAGE: The best known of all, where perceived rudeness or selfishness behind the wheel produces an angry, sometimes violent response from a fellow driver. Has resulted in murder and injury.

SUPERMARKET RAGE: Shoppers fight with others over 12-items, quick service queue.

TOLL BOOTH RAGE: Drivers who use the correct-change lane, then have to call for attendant. A Harbour Bridge special.

TAXI RAGE: People pushing in line at cab ranks, or walking a few metres ahead of the rank to flag vacant cabs.

POOL RAGE: Fanatical "lap nazis" get angry at slower swimmers in their lane. Cook + Phillip Park pool, as revealed in *The Daily Telegraph* yesterday, has put etiquette signs on all eight lanes.

SURF RAGE: Where a surfer is attacked for not sharing limited waves at a break.

NEWSAGENT RAGE: Newspaper buyers fed up with waiting behind Lotto players throw coins at newsagent staff.

FISHING SPORT RAGE: Where too many boats try to anchor on the one spot.

RAMP RAGE: Where selfish boat owners take up the entire boat ramp, then proceed to take forever to launch.

PETROL BOWSER RAGE: Drivers who fill up and leave car next to bowser.

VENDING MACHINE RAGE: When a product or coin gets stuck, people push and kick machine.

GOLF RAGE: Part-time golfers turned away because of dress, such as short socks or draw string pants.

Working through rights with a student group can be enlightening for all parties. When discussion turns from the rights of the individual to the rights of groups and the community, and the repercussions and responsibilities that rights incur for everyone, it can be a small step for some students, especially the boys, to recognise that their actions might affect others and that claiming their rights often impinges on the rights of another.

The following table is designed to assist staff working through this process. The top section could be completed prior to class discussion, the second part after varying thoughts have been proposed and argued. The numbers are there as a guide, and are not intended to be definitive or suggest a particular number. Before discussion, set a task that students can see has reasonable limits, one which they can achieve. This will encourage completion.

Rights

Individual	Community
1.	1.
2.	2.
3.	3.
4.	4.
5	5.
Individual	**Community**
1.	1.
2.	2.
3.	3.
4.	4.
5	5.

Figure 1.2   Responsibilities

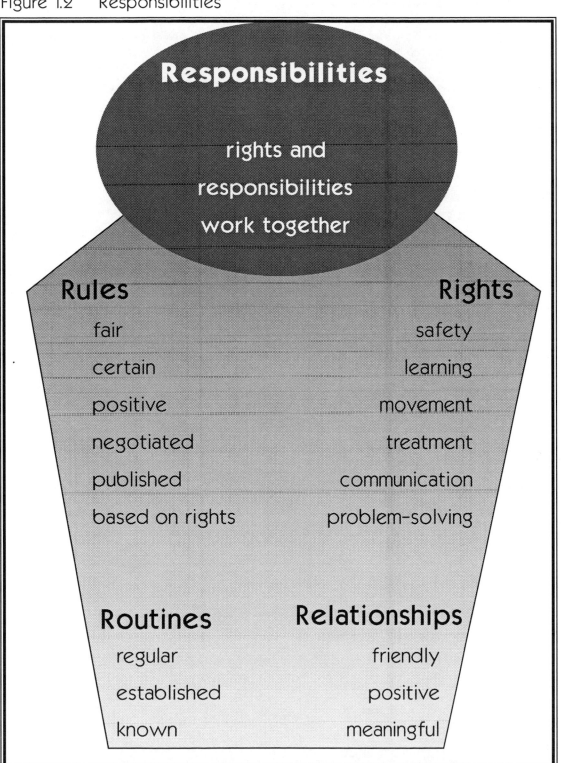

Responsibilities

rights and
responsibilities
work together

Rules   ### Rights

fair   safety

certain   learning

positive   movement

negotiated   treatment

published   communication

based on rights   problem-solving

Routines   ### Relationships

regular   friendly

established   positive

known   meaningful

Responsibilities

Boys will change when they are helped to understand themselves better, are affirmed and valued 'as they are' and are given the tools to feel safe and equal.[9]

Steve Biddulph

Responsibilities tie in with rights. All students have rights. All teachers have rights. All members of the community have rights. With these rights travel a group of responsibilities that ensure each person's rights do not excessively infringe on another's. As students progress through their school years, rules are used to develop and protect rights and responsibilities.

Every parent has heard children demanding their rights at some stage. Few have heard their offspring equally vociferously demand their responsibilities. In schools where there are large groups of students learning how to function in a community, not only do their rights need to be detailed but their responsibilities also need equal time. Some of our students are not quite as willing to accept responsibilities as much as rights. For this reason schools use rules to establish protocols that protect the rights of all students while, hopefully, developing students' awareness of their own responsibilities.

From the earliest years boys are referred to as being 'single focused' – especially on their own activities – disregarding others or not considering possible repercussions of their actions. This includes playing ball near glass windows, having a game of tips where people are trying to quietly relax, calling out in class to gain the teacher's attention, pushing in in lines at the canteen. The list is endless.

Boys are not the only perpetrators in this, but they seem to occupy more of our time and energy than do the girls. How is responsibility to be encouraged?

Let's recognise that this not a new phenomenon. Without wanting to go too far back in history, the jottings of Michael Brown[10] in the 1970s measuring masculinity amongst the black community in New York illustrate an attitude many teachers might be familiar with:

How much pain and violence you can inflict on another person

How many girls you can impregnate and not get married

How much reefer you can smoke, pills you can drop, and wine you can drink

How many times you can go to jail and come out 'unrehabilitated'

What kind of clothes you wear

How much money you have

What kind of car you drive

Some might argue that not much has changed in the last quarter of a century. While the creators of this piece were beyond school age, the excerpt illustrates an attitude towards responsibility. There does not appear to be much thought for consequences, the long-term or even the next day, and many of our boys in schools are developing such an attitude, though hopefully not to this degree, nor all of these actions. Taking risks without thought for the consequences, being self-centred, having a great deal of concern for one's own image – such characteristics are not exclusive to youth in classrooms.

Rights involve responsibilities. Allowing students to develop, take risks, and experience the many wonders that they should, involves developing responsibilities. For some students this takes more time and energy than for others. It seems the boys are there in force.

Reviewing rights and looking at responsibilities in schools and how schools are addressing these issues can bring about debate which few would choose to adjudicate. Using the succinct group of rights developed by Rogers[11] – safety, learning, treatment, movement, problem-solving and communication – a discussion of schools' development of students' responsibilities illustrates the variation and effort being made in this area. Many responsibilities overlap, just as rights can – and rules too.

The responsibilities associated with the right of safety focus on individuals ensuring their own safety and that of others in the school. This is often seen as a discipline/ welfare issue and treated as such. In recent years many schools, having recognised that existing discipline and welfare systems were not coping with changes in youth, have embraced Choice Theory[12] into their behaviour codes in an attempt to improve students' introspection and responsibility for their own actions. In many schools this has had a significant impact and this should be recognised. Restitution, as a separate issue, has been initiated in many schools, and this too has had much success. The aim is for individuals to be more responsible members of society, and for many of the boys we see in our playgrounds and classrooms this is the target at which we are aiming.

Some schools have embraced peer mediation rather than teacher-administered consequences as a method of reinforcing social responsibilities within the school community as well as reducing long-term teacher time spent on minor issues. Here too successes have been chalked up, with boys and girls finding clear rules and guidelines in the absence of teacher authority allows them to negotiate solutions to their problems. There has been some suggestion that peer mediation is more successful with primary-aged students than adolescents, and this may be correct. However, if younger students are developing these skills, then in the longer run there may be gains.

In the later years of the last millennium, bullying – the hidden school curriculum – has surfaced as an issue of safety and treatment. Boys are identified as perpetrators and

victims more readily than girls, and this might be due in part to both the nature and volume of male bullying. Olweus's pioneering work[13] nearly thirty years ago has launched many studies and as many programs to combat this most insidious aspect of school life. Varying researchers have commented on gendered bullying, homophobia, sexual harassment and just about every combination that can be contemplated, with some excellent programs being developed and implemented to address the situation in schools. This is still a young and complex study, though research has brought justifiable attention to it, centring largely on the activities of boys.

As Ken Rigby has found in his research on boys and bullying:

> It is certainly true that boys are more prone to bullying than are girls. Various explanations have been put forward. Some of these identify biological factors as paramount, for example the higher level of testosterone found among boys which is seen as accounting for their greater tendency to act aggressively. However, the role of physiological factors in mediating aggressiveness is complex and controversial and at this stage must be considered 'unproven'. At the same time it would be unwise to neglect the obvious fact that boys, especially in their teen years, are bigger and stronger than girls, and there is a greater opportunity for them to physically impose on others (including girls) who are less physically powerful than they are. It may also be the case that the greater degree of empathy (a factor that works against bullying others) which is generally found among girls owes something to biological factors that equip them to give birth to children and commonly results in them taking a more nurturing role in rearing of children.[14]

There do not appear to be easy solutions to this long-standing and often hidden problem, with power abuse readily demonstrated in many aspects of society and the intensity with which adolescents protect themselves from shame exacerbating the situation.

Other aspects of responsibilities for boys passing through our schools might be understanding their masculinity with issues of safety, treatment, learning, communication, and problem-solving emanating from this. Some schools have expanded personal health-type programs, drug education and child protection. The works of Browne and Fletcher[15], Biddulph[16] and West[17] have pioneered an approach that a few years ago was not apparent. Recognition of boys as likable, if not lovable – 'with their scruffiness, noisiness, in-your-face honesty and surprising capacity for tenderness and vulnerability'[18] (rather than seeing them as academically challenged behaviour problems), and understanding and tabling masculinity issues with boys, facilitates development of an ease with their own masculinity – aware of its lusts, angers and energies as well as desires for tenderness, camaraderie and belonging – without being coerced into social compliance.

In our schools teachers are straining to cope with the prescribed curriculum without adding the 'parenting' role often needed by students coming from dysfunctional families. Yet community expectations demand schools inculcate students with skills often not demonstrated at home, and encourage caregivers to take on a parenting role – regardless of suitability – as well as complete a rigorous academic agenda. And schools are responding in many ways.

Mentoring, in many guises, has sprouted as a means of assisting targeted youth not responding to existing welfare programs to accept their own and others' rights. Social skills, academia, organisation, anger management, even personal hygiene have been the basis for interventions aimed at supporting students through difficult periods. There can be great personal growth for all parties in these liaisons. In Browne and Fletcher's Boys in schools, Peter Ireland[19] reports on one such exercise on mentoring three senior secondary boys, while Peter Clarke recounts his experiences with primary students.[20] Both are isolated cases, but illustrate a range of options that schools are using to promote social responsibility amongst students.

Role modelling is part of every teacher's training. Younger students in particular pick up habits and mimic actions and mannerisms of teaching staff. Older students tend to mock quaint mannerisms or identifiable traits – but such mannerisms or traits seem to creep into their habits just as often. Whatever the age group, students notice how their teachers are acting and reacting. If there is an expectation that students respect the rights of others in their school, teaching staff must set an example. An expectation that learning and school is interesting and stimulating should be modelled consistently. Boys in particular will not respect teachers who they think 'cannot teach, shouldn't be allowed to teach, have lost interest in teaching, and who are unnecessarily, inequitably, inconsistently, and usually unsuccessfully, authoritarian.'[21] This can lead to a spiral of disaffection, resistance, resentment and anger culminating for some in retaliation at any cost. But students do respect 'good teachers' with whom 'they learn more, muck up less, work harder, improve their marks and want to stay on at school'.[22]

Schools encourage students to remain until the end of schooling, developing their skills in the sheltered school environment. Schools have recognised that traditional subjects may not be stimulating students, discouraging them from appreciating their right to learn and continuing on to the final years of schooling. Just as the 1970s revelations in girls' education saw encouragement of girls to explore new avenues with resultant increases in retention rates into senior school, there is recognition that current traditional subjects being offered are less than appropriate for today's youth. Courses aimed at workplace skills and responsibilities preparing students for the workforce have blossomed, as have courses catering for those students remaining at school who in previous years would have left to secure apprenticeships or employment positions not requiring post-compulsory schooling. There has been an impact on retention in senior years, but Slade and Trent's research indicates that boys think

school is not an adequate preparation for work because it is too rigid and antiquated, and much of the community debate regarding VET courses has not reached them.[23]

Involving students in monitoring their own progress has been used in primary schools for some time, but perhaps not so much in secondary. However, Judith Locke has documented a process of negotiating school reports with boys in her classes with improved acceptance of responsibility and outcomes for the students.[24]

Primary and infants programs such as Stop, Think, Do[25] progressively build social skills and awareness of others, and when implemented as whole-class or whole-school programs can have significant impact on behaviour issues. Simple and direct, modelled by staff using the same processes, certainly not gender-specific but with kinaesthetic lessons and concrete symbols, it lends itself to many smaller boys attempting to grasp these skills.

The range of actions schools are undertaking outside their traditional processes to retain boys in schools or to improve their academic and social outcomes while at school is probably at least as varied as the issues confronting schools. The following table is a useful check list.

Responsibilities	YES	NO
Am I satisfied with my interactions with all		
• colleagues?		
• students?		
• parents?		
Have I regularly demonstrated to students		
• interest in teaching?		
• interest in pupils?		
• respect for pupils?		
• respect for the school?		
• respect for my colleagues?		
Have I:		
• resolved problems with students rather than asserting authority to conclude a situation?		
• communicated with students rather than spoken at them?		
• ensured movement around the school/ class has not infringed on student learning?		
• had the safety of students as a primary concern in any organisation or supervision?		
• reviewed the learning opportunities I facilitate to ensure that a range of learning styles is addressed?		
• demonstrated respect for students even in disciplinary processes?		

Figure 1.3   Routines

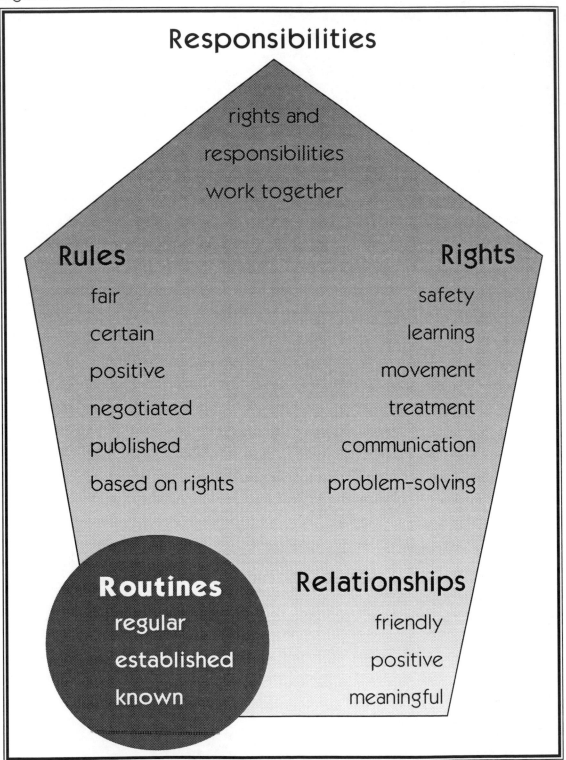

Responsibilities

rights and
responsibilities
work together

Rules
fair

certain

positive

negotiated

published

based on rights

Rights
safety

learning

movement

treatment

communication

problem-solving

Routines
regular

established

known

Relationships
friendly

positive

meaningful

Routines

Following a group of high school students from period to period on a given day as they go about their lessons will demonstrate the many different routines that students are expected to master. Even before they engage in the lesson the different routines they encounter may have an impact. At one classroom their bags will have to be neatly lined up along the wall outside the door, at the next they are taken inside the room, at the next put wherever they can find a space; caps are worn in one room, not in the next; swinging on chairs is okay with Teacher A but not with Teacher B; students line up and walk in together at science but walk in when they arrive for English; seating plans are enforced in one department but not in others, and the list goes on.

Teachers are not uniform in their classroom procedures, and it would be unrealistic for there to be an expectation of uniformity on all matters. However, when there is disparity there will be testing. Some of this may be from uncertainty regarding expectations, some may be wishing to challenge the staff member, some may be seeking the lowest common denominator (i.e. the easiest set of rules to follow), some may have yet other motivations.

However, a more uniform approach by all staff, even to student entry, may assist. When boys know what is uniformly expected at all classrooms, then the opportunity to claim lack of knowledge is reduced, as is the opportunity to test differences, and all students become more certain in their actions preparing for class. Some students, notably the boys, do not cope well with change and while many of their peers can cope with changes in procedure from one room to the next, for some boys' changes to routines present challenges and difficulties. These students are often quite unsettled and have probably had a tussle or two outside in the corridor or in the playground on the way to class, possibly been reprimanded by a staff member for these activities and arrive in class with an additional cocktail of emotions. The lesson has every possibility of being entertaining.

Routines in class affect students as well. When students are familiar with patterns of work then generally there is less likelihood of disruption. It is often the interchange, when students are unsure of what to do next, or when students have finished a task and are not programmed to move onto something else, when idle hands or uncertain minds seek alternative activities. When raising hands is usually expected prior to asking questions or answering them, but not always; when a class usually moves straight into their seats, but sometimes this doesn't happen; when wearing hats in class is okay, but then the teacher pulls up three people for not taking them off: these are the sorts of minor routine changes that unsettle some boys. When all are aware of expectations there is a collective sigh as the class settles on task.

Football practice

Visiting a football coach one night, the importance of routines was displayed. A national football figure was visiting the coach's home to run a clinic the next day for the local talent. We sat and discussed the need for some things to become routine for success on the field. During the discussion he asked the coach's son to stand up and walk over to a rug beside the fire. Somewhat bemused, the boy did so. The footballer thanked him and suggested he return to his seat. A while later, when the discussion had moved on to other topics he again asked the lad to go and stand on the rug. Wanting to impress, but still bemused, the boy complied and was again asked to return to his seat. The scenario was repeated once more. Later in the evening when the discussion had meandered over many topics the footballer called the lad's name again and without a word or hesitation the lad got up and stood on the rug. At that point the coach reiterated his point about routines. When players do not need to be told, when they know what they have to do, when doing it is automatic, it's a lot easier for the game to flow.

In the classroom, for many students, knowing what to do without having to think or be instructed reduces their indecision and allows more teaching time.

Watching the coaching sessions the next day, this coach demonstrated many techniques and skills, and it became apparent that players' performances improved as their confidence in expectations developed. When they were sure of what they had to do, they could focus on the skill. In the classroom, if routines are established so students have that confidence moving from one task to the next, knowing they are moving in the right direction, they can be more easily directed to learning.

Routines are established in classes where students know the process of answering questions without thinking about how to answer, when each student knows that after maths the class will move on to history, when each student knows that homework going out on Monday must be returned on Friday – the list goes on, but the message is familiar.

Students, particularly boys, need routines so they can feel comfortable with processes that are occurring. For this to occur the routines need to be

- *known* by everyone, not just the few
- *regularly* seen and enforced, so that there is consistency in application and no great time span between applications
- *established* as early as possible in the term and maintained

Routines Make a list of steps you wish students to do:	How do students know you want them to take these steps?
before entry to class	
immediately after entry to class	
when you are setting class tasks	
when you are handing out work	
when they finish tasks: • quickly • before others • as a group	

Discuss your routines at a faculty/department/grade/stage/ meeting.

Relating Routines

My routine	H.O.D.	Buddy	Other

How do your routines relate to other teachers of the same group of students?

Figure 1.4   Relationships

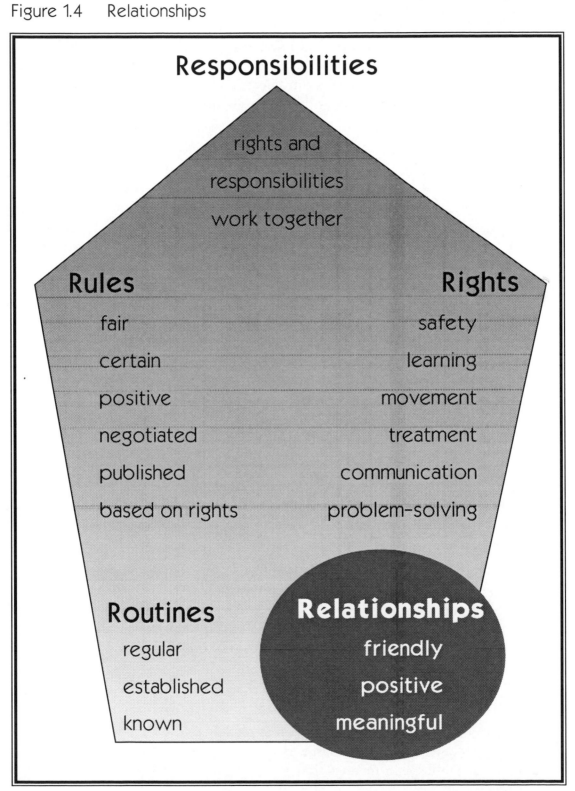

Relationships

A lot has been written about boys and relationships: how boys are not able or not willing to develop relationships, how boys have difficulty articulating their feelings and thoughts, how boys care more about objects rather than people. The adolescent period exacerbates issues for the boys themselves while their behaviours often attract attention from older heads.

William Pollack in his book *Real boys* discusses the confusion some of these boys are experiencing. By slightly changing a series of established tests he gave boys an opportunity to reveal conscious and unconscious attitudes they were grappling with. A sample of 150 adolescent boys scored well within the range of men and women who embrace 'the new masculinity' but were equally strong when they took the 'traditional male role' attitude scale. Pollack says, 'So when given the opportunity . . . these boys, without knowing it, revealed an inner fissure, a split in their sense of what it means to become a man.'[26] He cites research identifying boys as having more difficulty identifying happiness as a goal in life.[27] He has also used pictures and asked boys to interpret them. One example was a boy in a doorway of an old wooden house. Forty per cent of responses from adolescent boys focused on developmental themes and were neither positive nor negative (e.g. 'He just wants to sit and think in the shade' or 'A boy about to move from one place to another'), but 60 per cent of responses could be grouped into the following categories: the abandoned boy, the isolated boy, the boy as a victim. Pollack concludes, 'A boy contemplates his fate all alone. He's restless; he's lonely. He feels abandoned, perhaps stranded by his parents. He is frightened.'[28]

The adolescent boys that he is describing are going to have difficulty establishing meaningful relationships as they grapple with issues within themselves. But boys in junior years are increasingly attracting our attention for similar reasons. While this inner turmoil is occurring, these boys are sitting in our classrooms trying to focus on algebra, grammar, civics and history.

Unfortunately, too many come from households where adult male guidance through some of these quandaries is neither strong nor positive. 'Father hunger' and 'under-fathered' are terms coined by various writers regarding the absence of male role models for the growing generation in an attempt to explain this inner turmoil boys are ⬛⬛⬛⬛ Maybe they're right, but, whatever the origins, teachers need strategies ⬛⬛⬛ in class.

Teacher–student relationships

In the classroom, teachers can be both a role model and a catalyst; there can be the opportunity to demonstrate those aspects of social interaction that are regarded by society as acceptable, in a manner that boys can pick up without having the issues

'rammed down their throats', which does not promote acceptance. This can be achieved by examining social interactions without making them personal, so that boys can assess the issues (and their own interactions on a quiet and personal level, in their own time and manner) without embarrassment.

Recent research from Flinders University[29] gives a very strong message that relations with teachers lie at the heart of boys achieving their academic potential. Boys see their school problems primarily in terms of their relationships with teachers. They believe there are too many 'bad teachers' who 'don't ask', 'don't listen' and 'don't care'. Some 1800 students identified good teaching as of major importance to boys' success. They defined the good teacher as one who:

- listens to what you have to say

- respects you as a person, treats you like a friend, treats you as an adult

- is relaxed, enjoys his or her day and is able to laugh, especially at mistakes

- is flexible, adjusting rules and expectations to meet individuals' needs and particular circumstances

- explains the work, makes the work interesting, finds interesting things to do

- doesn't humiliate you in front of the class

- doesn't write slabs of work on the board to be copied

- lets you talk and move about the classroom

- doesn't favour girls, or boys who do what they are told

- doesn't keep picking on people who have a reputation, pushing them to retaliate

- doesn't mark you down because of your behaviour

- gives you a chance to muck up and learn from it

- doesn't keep telling you you're no good and should leave school[29]

The boys in this research:

- Identified sixty features constituting 'good' teaching, but in most schools they opined that less than ten per cent met the criteria. Teachers who are 'groovy', 'easy' or 'slack' are not considered good teachers.

- Thought good teachers could be male or female. They might be young or old – though 'young' is seen as a frame of mind rather than chronological age.

- Thought most boys value school largely, if not solely, for the social life

- Felt work in junior secondary years is boring, repetitive and irrelevant, that the expectations are low, there are no goals, no rewards and that assessment outcomes

have no real impact

- Observe that girls get a better deal at school, and this is uniformly considered a matter of fact

- Disagreed with attempts to focus on gender as a defining factor in their performance rather than teaching

- Think the curriculum is boring, repetitive and largely irrelevant. However, from their perspective, changing the curriculum cannot occur without changing the teachers

- Claim that the adult world is not listening and doesn't really care. This perception begins some time in the first year of secondary school and gets worse

- Failed to recognise programs directed at addressing declining boys' performance and retention as significant, or expressed the view that they were a waste of time, with the 'best' programs on offer to only a few – alternative programs such as STAR

Some anecdotal comment from the research:

If you get teachers that are really good, you can chat with them, have a good lesson, then you tend to get more work done. With teachers that are pricks to you, you tend not to like them, not try as hard, retaliate against them. (Year 11)

We'll get further with teachers like that . . . we're motivated to work if the teacher's relaxed. It makes it fun. We want to work. (Year 9)

I have a class . . . everyone in the class likes the teacher because he's relaxed. He gives us work that's interesting to do, and no-one stuffs around in his class because of that. (Year 9)

Recent media reports add weight to this research. The winner of the 2000 Victorian Teacher of the Year Award identified good teaching as caring for students (*Herald Sun*, 6 March 2001, p. 58) and concluded that this was the most outstanding attribute of the good teacher. Coincidentally, a group of Certificate III TAFE students were asked what makes a good teacher. While ability to interpret the curriculum was most commonly mentioned, empathy with students, flexibility in pedagogy and relationships with students, and an ability to enthuse and humour them, were high on the list. One student reported that a good teacher 'is concerned about you' (*The Australian*, 24 March 2001, p. 13).

For some of these students teachers may become role models, with qualities that society wishes our youth to have. By establishing friendly relations with students (rather than friendships) some of these qualities may be accepted by students.

Student relationships

Watch the kindergarten children and infants in the playground. The girls cluster in small groups talking, giggling, telling stories, communicating with their peers, while the boys are racing cars in the dirt under a tree, building tunnels and roads in the sandpit, aware of their peers and having some interaction with them but primarily focused on the adventure they are engaged in.

As they progress through primary school the girls will move in and out of friendship groups with lots of messages being carried backwards and forwards, 'best friends' being an important position with a great deal of communication and interaction among individuals, while boys will befriend the lad with the cricket bat, the boy who can run fastest or the best tackler in the playground. Much of the playground chatter will be about the game being played, the rules and how they can win rather than how they feel or their own persona. When boys do interact on a personal level, they are careful not to allow themselves to be the fall guy. Invitations to parties are given and received offhandedly, there are rituals in the change rooms when another boy is too close or is seen to be looking around, and discussions about girls, just like anything else, rarely focus on feelings or personality.

The work of three writers in this area sheds light on boys' relationships through the schooling years, demonstrating some of the complexities we face in the classroom. Professor Carol Martin's research found young children indicated a preference to play with others of the same sex from as early as two years old and this preference increased with age.[31] By age four, kids played with same sex peers about three times more often, and by age six the segregation happened eleven times more often. Her research identified some characteristics of gendered play:

Girls

- play in small groups

- are cooperative and agreeable

- do not interrupt each other as much

- are more likely to invent stories about dolls

- are usually relegated to leftover spots in the playground

Boys

- play in large, unstructured groups

- like to boast, hurl insults and challenge each other

- are disruptive and interrupt each other

- are more rough-and-tumble

- like body contact

Even as young students are entering our schools, a preference for play with their own sex is apparent and the play itself can be differentiated. Relationships will be developed as they progress through school, but the foundations of their initial contact can be identified as varying by gender.

Steve Biddulph makes the point that young boys don their personal armour as they near their school grounds, reducing their freedom of expression in favour of protection – becoming more macho to cope with playground issues. With their armour in place they 'do battle' for the day and return home shedding it as appropriate until they can be themselves again in their own environment.[32]

For youths in households with a caring environment this preparation and discarding of defences may be noticeable and even difficult. With age this transformation may prove more difficult, and where the household itself holds fears then the 'armour' will remain and any transformation may be even harder. A part of a boy's long-term character may well be established by peers and school culture.

In his book *Secret men's business* John Marsden argues that there are some steps that boys must take to reach manhood.[33] Not all will be resolved simultaneously, or near the same time, but there is a suggestion that some boys will be moving along the path while they are in schools. This is not a check list, nor a path with rites of passage, Marsden argues, but steps common to boys moving on to adulthood. As a series of challenges they provide an interesting framework through which to view some of the behavioural problems that appear for many boys around adolescence. (The comments beside each challenge are mine.)

- **Defeat your father.** This might be at some pursuit particular to the family, but the mental attitude needed for the challenge does not come without some honing. Some 'sparring partners' might be just the thing and teachers have many of the characteristics.

- **Leave school, leave home.** This involves building up responsibility. Many boys need to do this in small steps, starting with not being so dependent, and questioning those telling them what to do. Authority figures may be rebelled against without severe consequences. Before boys leave either school or home, they have begun to move along the path towards responsibility.

- **Test and demonstrate your courage.** This is not about driving at 140 kilometres per hour the wrong way down a one-way laneway at midnight without the lights on – but so many see that it could be, and take this as a demonstration of courage. Rather than debating, dancing or acting, it could be the kudos of 'standing up' to a teacher in class.

- **Earn your own money.** This is also about responsibility. If money is handed over without being earnt, boys don't understand responsibility. While many are doing this – Slade and Trent suggest 60 per cent of the boys they interviewed had employment outside school[34] – in school there are many restrictions imposed from above, with little responsibility taken by students.

- **Learn which rules are okay to break.** Most of us disregard the rules at some time, but boys have to know which ones can be broken without severe repercussions. This comes from maturity. In the meantime the learning curve bends through our classrooms.

- **Find what you believe in.** Marsden suggests a religion be advocated – it gives boys a direction in their lives. Direction is vital. Pollack cites research of girls being more able to identify long-term goals,[35] and whether it be religion or material gain, an incentive to succeed can only assist boys in their schooling.

- **Get your own voice.** Adults express their own thoughts. This is encouraged in schools, but so too are the directions, 'Write your essay this way . . .' or 'Your explanation of this piece of poetry should be like this'. For some reason, there is confusion.

- **Recognise your feelings.** Boys' failure to understand their own feelings cripples their personal development. This has gained significant attention as a male issue, and causes concern in the playground.

- **Experience success.** Achievable goals should be set. If goals are unachievable, the process will be perceived as not worthwhile, and anger and stress will surface. Research suggests boys have difficulty achieving literary goals throughout schooling.

- **Explore your feelings about death.** In our antiseptic world, youth do not have a real image of death. Many students have a fascination with death.

- **Don't have heroes.** When anyone worships a hero, it is implied that the hero is 'better' than them. This in itself is enough of a reason not to have heroes. When boys are emulating their heroes there are, too often, issues with school discipline and personal interaction.

- **Give.** Giving is one of the great pleasures of being an adult. Children can give, but it is usually not something of their own. If they buy something with money given to them – rather than earned – it is a transfer from the original donor rather than from the juvenile. Something given, when it is earned by the donor, is the precinct of the adult. Recognition of the 'gift' of time is important.

This list is thought-provoking for any teacher. When considered with the work of Martin and Biddulph, the suggestion is that boys' characteristics will be reinforced by their activities as they progress through school. Young boys are increasingly seeking same sex peers with whom to associate. Actions in the schoolyard and outside school are aimed at giving maximum credibility to the 'armoured lad' as he negotiates the playground. The role he adopts will reinforce the culturally acceptable. It might even be better to exaggerate some of the characteristics rather than question them or not comply. Opening up to express feelings and dialogue about abstract thoughts doesn't

fit the model. The likelihood of openly seeking meaningful communication on important matters with teachers in their high school years diminishes as some of these characteristics are developed, coinciding with gradual movement down the path from maturity to manhood, and the conflict this brings to the classroom.

Yet when asked in an impersonal, non-confrontational manner, boys want people to be 'interested' in them. Boys find schools to be unhappy places and most do not want to spend extended periods where they perceive success to be beyond them. Their glimmer of hope is teaching staff who have their interests at heart. They care if the teacher cares. They want 'relationships' with their teachers – ones where the leader excites their minds and gives real and worldly guidance that is not stultified by bureaucracy. Neither chronological age nor sex are intrinsic barriers; it is the quality of the offering that is important.

It is important to note the following:

- Some students will work better with teachers who show an interest in them rather than the subject matter.

- Some students may not have successful role models within their family or extended family circles.

- Some students seek role models.

What can we do?

All teachers have noticed young boys 'batting like Mark Waugh', or charging the line like 'the Chief', copying the older boys in the playground or discussing and mimicking actions seen in film or advertisements. Teachers too are grist to the mill. Primary children and infants can often be seen 'walking like Mr Jones' or imitating the hand movements of Ms White. In these years, when kids are in school, their teachers are the raw material for them for a good part of their day.

Modelling the sort of behaviours that are expected might encourage some of these young boys to pick up on some aspects demonstrated.

Show interest in students' out-of-school activities

The boys are usually all too keen to discuss their sporting victories, and, with a bit of cajoling, explain their losses. Everyone gets a duck from time to time; no full-back has stopped every attacking move; even Pat Rafter has been beaten by an unseeded player. But what else happened on the day? A few good fielding efforts? A run down the line evading a couple of tackles? Two aces? Something positive? Saw a good accident on the way home? Played down the creek in the mud all afternoon still in their whites and Mum got *how* cross?

If boys get a ton, then this is good. Celebrate their success. Each success that is discussed is a chance to build rapport. If they want to tell you, then you are well on the way.

Many boys will not be interested in traditional sport. They may be more interested in computer games, art shows or theatre. It might be hard to be enthusiastic when the topic is Orks or ice-skating, but your interest rather than your knowledge is what is being tested.

Listen – some students just want to be heard

For some, the chance to be listened to is a rare opportunity. An adult with time and interest is heaven sent. The chance to spend meaningful time in discussion with adults can be precious. While it may be time-consuming, in the long run it can be time very well spent. Following is a check list teachers may like to use.

Student's name	Sport/ interest/ hobby	Likes	Hates	Something shared with you

Figure 1.5   Rules

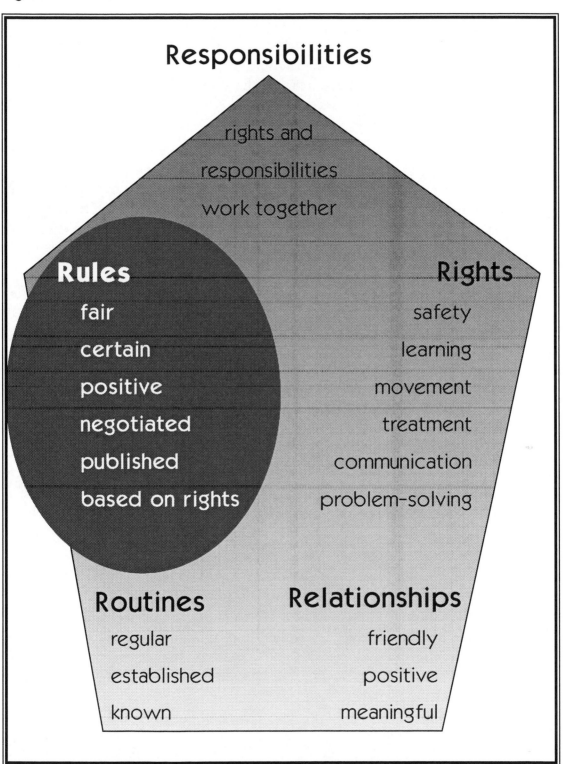

Rules

Often there is the assumption made that students know how to behave. Many certainly do. Unfortunately, for various reasons, some do not. Some choose to behave in a manner that adversely affects the learning and rights of other students. Over the past decades students have become increasingly aware of their rights, and when staff approach class members about class members' actions they often take the opportunity to raise rights in their defence.

However, the reciprocating responsibilities are often readily forgotten or stored in a memory compartment that is only opened with pressure. If the classroom is to be a safe, cooperative learning environment, all the players need to know their roles and the expectations others have of them. This can be done by establishing rules from the start of each year, semester or term, delineating the playing field so that everyone can begin with established parameters. Clear guidelines for transgressions will assist both students and teachers, reducing personal issues and indecision.

Watch boys establishing rules for their lunchtime games. They will spend more time than girls establishing and refining rules for an activity that has their interest. Yet often when there is the opportunity to engage in classroom rule formation they are quiet. The classroom may have less interest than their playground activities. It may involve some encouragement for the boys to be positively involved at the start. It might also give teachers an insight into how boys view their classes. It is important for the boys to be involved, as the perceived 'picking on them' syndrome is more difficult to raise if they have been involved in the process itself. This is also a strengthening of boys' commitment to the classroom itself and encourages their participation.

Boys will test the rules, argue about their construction, point out inconsistencies, turn the rules against the system and examine the teacher's application for fairness and discrimination. Classroom practitioners should have a clear picture of acceptable and unacceptable behaviour in their minds before they enter the classroom and take steps to negotiate these with their classes, covering consequences or procedures that will occur if rules are broken. Students, too, need the opportunity to express their expectations and desires. Communication needs to be established from the beginning, not just talked about.

Rules are the framework within which the classroom can begin to function as a safe learning place. They are like the ropes around a boxing ring (many teachers have probably gone home some days feeling they have 'gone a few rounds'), they are flexible and define the playing surface.

Steve Biddulph[36] argues that boys want to know:

- What are the rules?

- Who is in charge?

- Will the rules be applied fairly?

By establishing a clearly understood, negotiated set of appropriate classroom rules the first question could be answered. Their consistent application and reinforcement with clear, logical consequences should help with the second two. Biddulph says, 'Boys act tough to cover up their fear. If someone is clearly the boss, they relax. But the boss must not be erratic or punitive. If the person in charge is a bully, the boys' stress levels rise, and it's back to the law of the jungle. If the teacher . . . is kind and fair (as well as being strict), then boys will drop their 'macho' act and get on with learning.'[37]

One boy's account

One day at school we had a substitute teacher for one of our lessons. She came in and basically said, 'Sit down and shut up. Oh! and listen also.' I was actually surprised to see the girls in the class do pretty much exactly that, while the boys were sort of stunned. We really didn't move much at all towards opening our books or obeying her orders, except for one or two 'goody-goodies'. After a while we started lisening to her, although no-one really mucked up. About half way through the class she said she was 'very disappointed with the behaviour of the top class' although no-one had really done anything at all (except the occasional murmur while working). When she said that the girls kept on working, but every single boy stopped and looked up at her. Straight after she had finished her 'disappointment' speech, one of the boys stood up and said directly back to her, 'Well, we're pretty disappointed with you too, Miss!' in a normal speaking tone. It was sort of like he was the self-appointed spokesperson for the general feeling of the class. When he said that, every single student in the room stopped work and either grinned or applauded.

Year 8[38]

Boys particularly will challenge the rules, but if there is consistency, reasonable rules will be accepted. In secondary schools where students move from specialist teacher to specialist teacher they may be confronted with many variations of 'the rules' and just as many variations in enforcing them. Learning teams, stage groups or teachers of particular classes could find methods such as meeting as a group at the start of term, formulating agreed practices and negotiating class rules as a group helpful towards overcoming some of these inconsistencies.

Rules need to be revisited regularly not only to reinforce but to determine their relevance. Just as the boys change the rules of their playground games to suit new conditions or unexpected circumstances, classroom rules can be dynamic. Rules set at the start of the year may not be as relevant for the group by the end, as they have moved on in their development and teachers and students have become more familiar with expectations within the setting.

When boys relax – when they feel they will be listened to – and see that they can influence the situation, rule reviews may become positive experiences as their sense of ownership and participation increases.

Negotiation

None of us likes to be told how we are going to act, what we are going to do or when we are going to do it without having at least some input of our own. The media bombards our youth with movies demonstrating the fallibility and corruptness of various institutions, lauding the underdogs who question authority and win justice. If the classroom 'authority' (the teacher) appears similar to these media images, imposing rules without negotiation, an Erin Brockovich-style army might well materialise, ready to test this authority. When there is to be group interaction, group determination of acceptable behaviour can only increase the chances of compliance.

Boys particularly will react to being told the rules. Whether it be vestiges of the warrior image, their macho image being questioned or a competitive edge, it is important to remember that even when the rules are clearly elucidated they will still be seen as part of a playing field for competing with authority.

Enforcement must be fair and impartial or else the angst generated will be more personal than against the institution. If the rules are perceived as those of the teacher rather than the class, then additional resentment can occur.

Rights as a basis

It should be possible to explain and understand each rule as protecting rights of students. Illustrating the responsibilities of students to support others' rights just as their own should form a part of the negotiations.

Consequences for transgressions should be included as well. If students understand the rule and the reason for its existence, the consequences for breaking the rule, and have participated in establishing both the rule and the consequence, then the probability these rules will be accepted will only increase.

Publishing rules

If rules are poorly phrased, ambiguous, not understood, inappropriate, not seen and not regularly reinforced, then 'testing' and 'challenges' will increase. Some students will test the barriers because they are uncertain, some because they may not understand, some to gain attention and some for the fun of it. By clearly expressing rules, displaying them, regularly reinforcing them, and ensuring they are understood, some of this will diminish.

Classroom rules should be displayed separately with one rule per display and each display a different colour. Each rule should be big enough to be easily seen in any corner of the room. When each rule is easily readable from every point in the room, stands out from other display material and is separate from all other rules, reminding students of the rules becomes an easier task.

This adds an intervention level for teachers: catching a student's eye and pointing or nodding in the direction of the rule. For many boys the intervention of the teacher is embarrassing and invites a 'fight or flight' response. This low-key intervention can enable a teacher to remind a student that they are breaking a rule without having to attract the attention of anyone other than the student involved. If all the rules are together, in a single place on a wall, or behind the door, it can be difficult to indicate which rule is being nudged without some interchange.

Regular movement of rules displayed in this manner encourages revisiting them. Students, particularly boys, notice when the visual stimulus of the room changes. Moving the coloured rules around the room on a regular basis will facilitate some discussion, and the opportunity to revisit the rule and the rights it protects in a short discussion serves as reinforcement.

Certainty

Most of us need to have information repeated to us from time to time. Drivers are constantly reminded of speed limits, yet police officers continually catch people speeding. It is unlikely that there is a school in which teachers have not had to be reminded to have programs, marks, reports or assessment tasks ready by certain dates. Students also require regular reinforcement of the rules. When the rule is forgotten or is just being ignored, reinforcement in a least intrusive manner to obtain the desired outcome is required.

It is the certainty of correction rather than the severity of the consequence that has the greatest impact over the long-term.

Using the display method discussed above, reinforcement can be a regular, non-confrontational event. Reinforcement is not 'picking on' the student who may be off-task but generating whole-class compliance.

Boys in particular will notice inconsistent application of rules. We have all heard the cry, 'What about so-and-so?'. If students are allowed to circumvent one rule while another is reinforced, they will probably take up this case. Certainty of application is vitally important if boys are to be aware of equity in the class.

Many discussions with adolescent boys about school will quickly turn to 'teachers picking on them' and 'favouring the girls', and many preadolescent youths echo this call. There is often resentment towards both administrators and female students when

the boys perceive that they have been treated unfairly. Consistent application in a fair and even-handed manner will help to break down this attitude.

In all fairness

Before teachers set out to involve students in rule negotiations they should have a firm knowledge of the protocols within their key learning area, faculty, stage group, year group, department, or subject area in the school. Discussion with a buddy teacher, executive, or experienced teacher can well be a guide through pitfalls.

Rules should be fair to the entire group and to individuals within the group. When adolescents are given the opportunity they will often 'hang 'em high', but teachers need to ensure that rules and consequences apply to all students in the group not just the targeted few.

Positive statements

All rules should be stated positively. Some students will have difficulty understanding what is expected. Some will challenge. Some will seek loopholes. An instruction such as 'Do not run' does not indicate that cartwheels, walking on hands, skipping and various other ways of moving from one place to another are not also appropriate. 'We will walk' at least reduces the possibility for variations.

My Rules

Right	Responsibilities	Rule

Further reading

Arndt, B., *Taking sides*, Random House, Sydney, 1995.

Berman, S., *Making choice theory work in a quality classroom*, Hawker Brownlow Education, Melbourne, 1998.

Biddulph, S., *Raising boys*, Finch, Sydney, 1997.

Biddulph, S., *Stories of manhood*, Finch, Sydney, 2000.

Biddulph, S., Fletcher, R., & Edgar, D., *Leadership in boys' education*, University of Newcastle, 1998.

Blum, D., *Sex on the brain*, Viking, New York, 1997.

Bosch, K., *Planning classroom management for change*, Hawker Brownlow Education, Melbourne, 2000.

Boys in schools journal, University of Newcastle.

Eberhart-Wright, A., *Rules: both stepping stones and stumbling blocks*, NHSA journal, vol. 13, no. 1, p. 47–49, 1994.

Edgar, D., *Men, mateship, marriage*, Harper Collins, Sydney, 1997.

Grant, I., *Fathers who dare win*, PA, Sydney, 1999.

Grey, J., *Men are from Mars, women are from Venus*, Harper Collins, New York, 1992.

Hartman, D., *I can hardly wait till Monday*, University of Newcastle, 1999.

Hawkes T., *Boy oh boy: how to raise and educate boys*, Prentice Hall, Sydney, 2001.

Holborrow, B., *Kids*, Random House, Sydney, 1999.

Hornby, N., *About a boy*, Victor Gollancz, London, 1998.

Keen, S., *Fire in the belly*, Bantam, New York, 1991.

Lamb, K., *Girls are from Saturn, boys are from Jupiter*, Piccadilly, London, 1998.

Mackay, H., *Generations*, Macmillan, Sydney, 1997.

MacNaughton, G., *Rethinking gender in early childhood education*, Allen & Unwin, Sydney, 2000.

Newberger, E., *The men they will become*, Bloomsbury, London, 2000.

Philips, A., *The trouble with boys*, Pandora, Glasgow, 1993.

Rogers, L., *Sexing the brain*, Wiedenfield & Nicolson, London, 1999.

Shores, D., *Boys and Relationships*, University of Newcastle, 1995.

Walker, J. C., *Louts and legends*, Allen & Unwin, 1988.

Webb, J., *Junk male*, Harper Collins, Sydney, 1998.

Notes

1. B. Rogers, *Behaviour management*, Scholastic, Melbourne, 1995.

2. D. Campbell, 'Teachers to be insured for murder on the job', *Sydney Morning Herald*, 28–29 July 2001.

3. J. Baird, 'You're out: principals tell students', *Sydney Morning Herald*, 1 June 2001.

4. M. Cole, 'State hides school discipline crisis', *Courier-Mail*, 1 March 2000.

5. N. Burke, 'Expelled student returns with knife', *The Daily Telegraph*, 12 December 2001.

6. G. Noonan, 'Boys take honours – in wagging', *Sydney Morning Herald*, 7 June 2001.

7. Australian Institute of Criminology, 'Australian crime: facts and figures', Canberra, 2000.

8. R. Rodda, 'Angry city', *The Daily Telegraph*, 3 July 2001.

9. S. Biddulph, *Boys in schools*, eds Browne, R. & Fletcher, R., Finch, Sydney, 1995, p. ix.

10. M. Brown, *Image of a man*, East Publications, New York, 1976, p. 6.

11. ibid., p. 79.

12. W. Glasser, *Control theory: a new explanation of how we control our lives*, Harper & Rowe, New York, 1984.

13. D. Olweus, *Aggression in schools: bullies and whipping boys*, Wiley, New York, 1978.

14. K. Rigby, 'Boys & bullying', *Boys in schools bulletin*, vol. 4, no. 4, pp. 14–21.

15. R. Browne & R. Fletcher, *Boys in schools*, Finch, Sydney, 1995.

16. S. Biddulph, *Raising boys*, Finch, Sydney, 1997.

17. P. West, 'Boys' underachievement in school: some persistent problems and some current research', *Issues in educational research*, vol. 9, no. 1, 1999.

18. S. Biddulph, *Boys in schools*, eds Browne, R. & Fletcher, R., Finch, Sydney, 1995, p. ix.

19. P. Ireland, 'Nurturing boys, developing skills', *Boys in schools*, eds Browne, R., & Fletcher, R., Finch, Sydney, 1995, pp. 212–222.

20. P. Clarke, 'I'll get you at lunch', *Boys in schools*, Browne, R. & Fletcher, R., eds, Finch, Sydney, 1995, pp. 168–177.

21. M. Slade, 'Listening to the boys', *Boys in schools journal*, vol. 4, no. 1, pp. 10–18.

22. ibid., p. 15.

23. ibid., p. 18.

24. J. Locke, 'Reports with rapport', *Boys in schools bulletin*, vol. 3, no. 4, pp. 19–20.

25. L. Peterson, & A. Ganoni, 'Stop, think, do', ACER.

26. W. Pollack, *Real boys*, Scribe, Melbourne, 1999, p. 166.

27. ibid., p. 173.

28. ibid., pp. 171–2.

29. Slade & Trent, 'What the boys are saying: examining the views of boys about declining rates of achievement and retention', *Boys in schools bulletin*, vol. 4, no. 1.

30. ibid., p. 14.

31. Arizona State University research published in *Journal of social and personal relationships* and reported in *The Sydney Morning Herald*, 21 May 2000.

32. S. Biddulph, *Raising boys*, Finch, 1997.

33. J. Marsden, *Secret men's business*, Pan Macmillan, Sydney, 1998.

34. ibid., p. 16.

35. W. Pollack, *Real boys*, Scribe, Melbourne, 1999.

36. S. Biddulph, *Raising boys*, Finch, Sydney, 1997, p. 40.

37. ibid., p. 41.

38. Interview with a high school student from Dubbo.

part2

Inside the door

Specific classroom techniques

Below is a list of things to consider in your classroom:

- As a technique, conditioning is very important and effective. It includes the following types of behaviour:

  - walking into class in a set way

  - sitting down

  - getting out books

  - starting work

  - being polite

  - showing care towards others

  - showing that you have listened

- Provide a predictable, stable and safe environment – a routine – so that people will know what will happen next.

- Utilise conditioning principles. This includes the following:

  - reward expected behaviour

  - apply predetermined consequences to, or ignore, unacceptable behaviour.

- Establish clear class goals

  - set class-determined goals on walls

  - have class ethos

  - regularly refer and reinforce the above

- Have work fully planned in advance, but be flexible enough to vary the procedure if necessary. Here it is important to:

  - know the material

  - know where you are heading

  - know your students

- Pitch work at a level that is reasonable for your students; expectations must be reasonable.

- Shorten periods of concentration with difficult students; intersperse their work with varied activities. As a rule of thumb, the more disturbed the student, the shorter the attention span.

- Aim at reducing anxiety by using a firm but calm approach. Angry and/or frightened teachers heighten the anxiety of students with behavioural difficulties. Avoid confrontation and showdown situations whenever possible.

- Standards, expectations and limits must be clearly defined and consistently upheld by everyone, not just the classroom teacher. Share responsibility, especially for major behavioural problems.

- Think positively towards the student. Accept the student, do not accept the behaviour. Do the following:

  - expect improvement

  - look for the student's good points

  - base work around these strengths

  - avoid negative thinking about yourself and/or the student

- Be fair interpreting rules and be scrupulously consistent.

- Establish your role. Teachers:

  - facilitate learning

  - are responsible

  - are in charge

  - are there to help

- Give clear, firm directions with clear guidelines. Students respond better to overt, firm, clear guidelines. These reduce:

  - double bind situations

  - emotional blackmail

  - damaged perceptions

Figure 2.1   Acknowledging behaviour

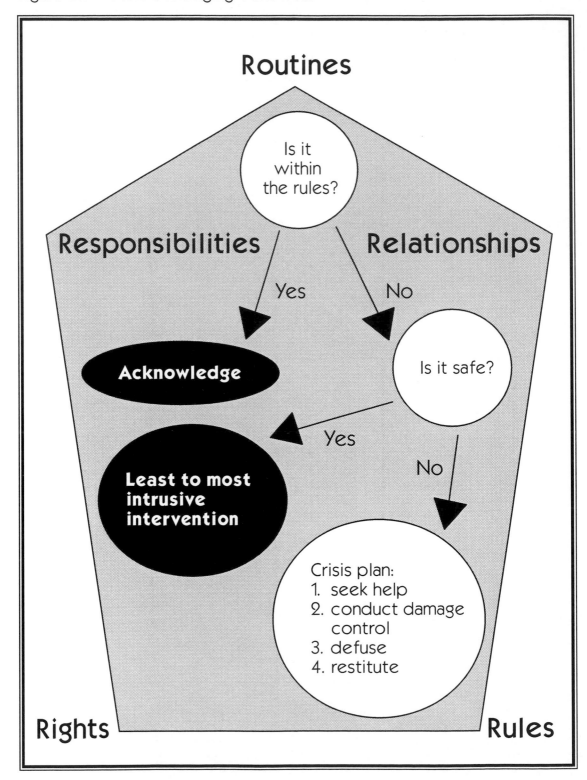

Positive consequences

Just as the rules of the classroom should be checked against the school rules, as well as those applying to a key learning area, department, faculty or grade, so too should the positive rewards component.

In the perception of many boys, schools are very good at telling them what *not* to do, or, more explicitly, catching them doing something and handing out a punishment. We may not be very good at showing students *what* to do. Students coming from dysfunctional homes, or households where expected behaviours at school are not the norm, can find it difficult when there are negative consequences at school for behaviour that is acceptable at home.

Often, negative consequences are meted out in the belief that students do know the 'correct' actions and choose not to comply – and this may be true – but also in the belief that the negative consequence will guide the student back towards the 'correct' action – and this may be true, too. It may also be true, however, that students are confused about the 'correct' action when they are faced with contrasting regimes – school and home – and in moments of stress the learnt behaviours from their relatively short time in school may be overshadowed by those behaviours acceptable in their home environment. Additionally, the negative consequences schools use might be relatively minor in comparison to the consequences applied in the home environment. A serious school consequence (in itself rather than as a step in a process, which many boys do not appreciate until it is really spelt out), might be trivial on their scale.

Reliance on punishment to manage boys' behaviour produces some interesting effects. Those old enough to admit being students during the times when corporal punishment was used will be able to remember boys who proudly stood up for a caning so that they could jot it into their 'book'. Competition for the most 'cuts' in a day, week or term raged in most schools with kudos from, and competition with, their peers often being stronger influences than the physical pain from the punishment. Even those not entering these competitions could rank teachers on their effectiveness with the cane, and student behaviour was often modified by teachers' ranking in the 'order of merit'. A more effective encounter produced longer periods of 'good' behaviour; a less painful session could be laughed off with a few mates in a short time.

Fear is the tool used to maintain order. The 'culprit' is encouraged to maintain better behaviour only through fear of further reprehension. If the punishment is overused, or students become overly familiar with it, it may have a diminished or limited impact.

A simple model of this is represented below.

Graph 2.1   Changing behaviour

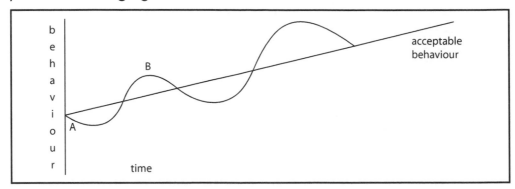

Students' general behaviour starts around A, remembering that some students will always be above the line due to their dedication, upbringing, wanting to please or internal strength, and might rarely, if ever, have negative consequences applied to them.

Over time, some students will test the rules. Behaviour deteriorates below the line showing acceptable behaviour. Negative consequences are applied, and recalcitrant students pull up their socks and comply. In fact, these students probably behave even better than previously. (Think of the primary school boy who, when wanting to please, sits up straight with his chest puffed out and does just anything to please. Usually he can't maintain this for very long, and moves to position B.)

After a while, this wears a bit thin. If there are no rewards and only the dislike of negative consequences to sustain the effort of behaving especially well, memory fades and it's testing time again. Behaviour deteriorates, but only when it falls below the line of acceptability are negative consequences applied. By this stage, students will be a bit more familiar with the consequences, and these may need to be intensified to yield the same reaction. And so the cycle of ever-increasing consequences and behaviour fluctuation begins. Without positive consequences to give students an incentive to behave in a manner deemed acceptable, boys especially – in an environment that is not their first option – will quickly feel that they are being had and will seek alternative attractions: entertainment, power plays, competitive interaction, revenge for prior incidents.

By also using rewards, students have an incentive to maintain their behaviour above the norm or at least a target to help them stay above the line.

The aim is for behaviour to look more like Graph 2.2. By using positive consequences to reward behaviour, when students achieve or surpass the 'acceptable behaviour' line, there is an incentive to remain there, other than the fear of negative consequences.

Graph 2.2   Closer to ideal

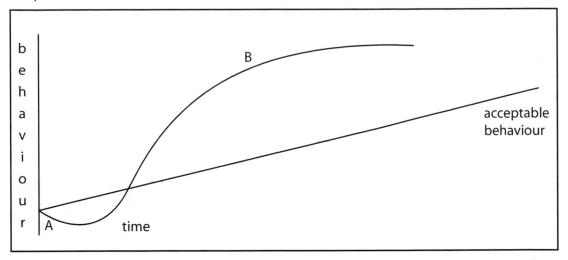

Whenever this topic comes up, teachers raise concerns about:

- the student who is regularly difficult but has performed an isolated incident of merit
- how the elite are over-rewarded
- . how the middle years of secondary schools are under-rewarded
- how the middle achievers do not attract attention

Students notice it too. The other discussion point regularly raised is rewarding students for 'normal' behaviour. Why reward students for doing something that is expected? Perhaps a quick review of our own feelings when someone thanked us for doing a 'good job' or 'making an effort' would be sufficient. If that pleasant feeling can be generated for students in the classroom, it can only assist their time there.

After a few terms or years, boys in high schools have often 'spat the dummy' over rewards. They can see the inconsistencies, they perceive they have not had a 'fair go' and they withdraw in many different ways with many different attitudes, including the idea that it is no longer 'cool' to receive awards, 'They don't mean nuthin'', 'I don't want that' and 'This sux'.

Achievement reduces until their final years. Suddenly, a good school report has value. There is a purpose to gaining 'merits', 'points' or whatever. Some of the boys start playing the game again. Unfortunately for some, their final year of schooling is not the final year offered and they are still in the testosterone- and rebellion-fuelled, 'I hate school' frame of mind and they have difficulty managing the seesaw of emotion versus outcome, as well as the consistency and sustained effort required to improve their reports. Too often they leave with unsatisfactory statements of their time in school and unsatisfactory memories. Perhaps, in the short-term, this quote illustrates the

situation:

> *Boys are always delightful in February and March, distressing towards the end of first term, beyond hope in August, exasperating in November, when inequity always comes to light, and again not so bad in December, when one says good-bye to so many of them with regret.*
>
> Sir James Darling – Headmaster, Geelong Grammar

If positive consequences are to have an impact, the rewards offered must have significance to students. Stickers, merit cards and material rewards may cajole some students but not all, just as development of intrinsic values will be appropriate for some. Negotiation with students when establishing class rules can lead to positive consequences that are relevant to the particular student body. There are likely to be varying expectations and desires within the group, and if these are demonstrated, an appropriate system might be developed. Often students seek additional library time, extra time on computers, additional playtime on special equipment, the whole class enjoying a special activity that is not on the timetable, just as much as others may value material rewards.

As a reward, praise is quick and easy to give, but sincerity is important. Comments like, 'This is the second best piece of work I've seen today', followed by, 'and I haven't seen the best piece yet', might be intended as a bit of a joke, but for many it effectively discourages them. If it is a good piece of work, let the student know, without 'holding a few marks in hand' or waiting for a better piece.

If the best mark any student will be awarded is 7 out of 10 (if one assumes that no-one can achieve 10 out of 10, only the teacher could achieve 9 out of 10, and other teachers could get 8 out of 10), the student questions the value of striving for the best result.

When giving praise, let students know what is good. A quick passing comment such as, 'that's good' as a teacher passes a student's desk may be intended as praise and for some students may be satisfactory, but just what was it about the piece of work that attracted the teacher's eye, and just which aspect of the work was 'good'? Some students in this position have little idea that the comment might have referred to the picture and not the content that had taken three hours of library research after school. By letting students know what is 'good', students receive better feedback about where their strengths are and what needs work.

As with a negative consequence, the certainty of a reward's occurrence is important. Students rapidly lose interest in promised rewards that do not materialise, or take too long in their time frame to occur. Rewards that are promised 'next week' or even 'tomorrow' might be too far away in their minds, and, too often (which might only be once or twice), circumstances prevent completion of the deal. Interest is lost.

Rewards – some reasonable guidelines

Rewards must be:

- **Reliable.** When a reward is earned it needs to be forthcoming – quickly and surely. Just like in Nintendo games.

- **Achievable.** Expected behaviours must be within the capacity of students. If boys are going to participate, they need to feel that they have a chance at succeeding. Secondary schools often have 'level' systems which offer rewards for varying activities or behaviours. If the expected behaviours are not achievable by some students, then those 'levels' are not seen as relevant and boys will withdraw from the system.

- **Simple.** The more complex the system the greater the chance of inconsistency, variations in application and, in short, ineffectiveness. Boys especially like to know how things work. To keep their focus, the system needs to be able to be explained quickly so they can see their opportunities. If they can see difficulties or blockages, they will withdraw.

- **Transparent.** Records kept in secret, rewards not seen, a system that is not understood and is perceived to play favourites will discourage boys from participating. They want to understand how it works and be able to see that each step is correct. Boys have a strong sense of justice, and if the system has an air of injustice they will not participate. It has to be seen to be just.

- **Effective.** To attract effort, rewards must be desired. If the rewards gained through any system are not desired by the target population, then the students' willingness to try is reduced.

- **Continuous.** When the early levels of reward systems focus on the classroom, but ensuing levels demand additional activities, the classroom behaviour may be seen as irrelevant once the initial levels are achieved. If the system is to be effective, classrooms should be the focus throughout.

- **Equitable.** If students observe one group rewarded for behaviours they too have been exhibiting but are not similarly rewarded, their sense of injustice will encourage them to withdraw.

Following is a chart of possible rewards for classroom behaviour. Praise is the first reward in each category. For many boys, this is extremely important, though few would openly acknowledge it. Behaviourists have pointed out the need for many more positive relative to negative interventions for people to remain on an even balance. Boys respond to those little positive reminders. Not the over-the-top embarrassment-causing praise, but the quiet recognition. Regularly administered.

Action or instruction	Possible positive consequence
Be quiet in class	• praise • period to talk at end of activity • choice of class activity at end of lesson • non-verbal reinforcement • time to express ideas
Raise hand to talk	• praise • being asked to answer • recognition of rule compliance
Complete assigned work	• praise • work marked promptly • recognition by showing others, e.g. the principal
Work in a group	• praise • free time when group has completed task • choice of next activity • choice of next group
Listen when others are talking	• praise • opportunity to speak to class
Complete homework	• praise • work read or displayed • note to caregiver (if appropriate)
Keep hands to self	• praise • input into seating arrangement
Care for equipment	• praise • input into next topic • input on order of work
Arrive at class on time	• praise • choice of seat

My class rules

Rule	Positive consequence

Figure 2.2   Consider the method of intervention

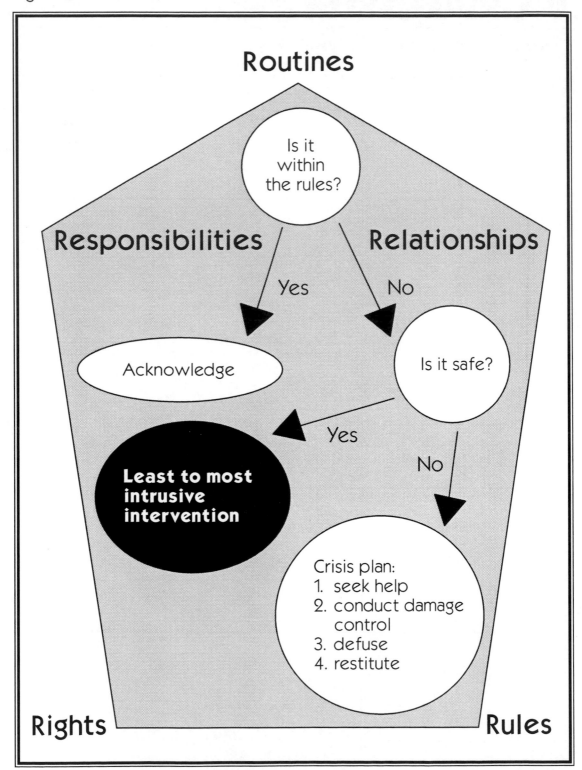

Negative consequences

When a student exhibits bad manners, writing out lines or giving detention may not be a logical consequence. Consequences should be clearly stated; there should be no varying sets of consequences dependent on sex, name, smile, time of day, hair colour, parents' occupation or any other variable, and they should be relevant to the action. (See Figure 2.3.)

Students will quickly determine if consequences are equitable. Ask any 14- or 15-year-old whether consequences for girls are the same as those meted out for boys, and the vast majority of responses will describe inequity. Boys often feel they are badly done by; many recognise that they have earned the wrath of their teacher, or the school's discipline system, but feel picked on. Consistency is vital.

Teachers who have prepared their behaviour management processes and negotiated these with their students usually find that applying consequences is less traumatic than for those staff not so prepared. When prepared, if a student transgresses and is apprehended, both the teacher and the student are aware of the consequence and it is a matter of course. Someone not in teaching once put it, 'It is not personal. This is business.' It is not a matter of liking or disliking the student. The behaviour is being addressed. On an occasion when staff are not adequately prepared, their own flustered feelings may be demonstrated and this can only aggravate the situation.

When applying consequences teachers need to be firm and unambiguous. If there is a chink perceived, boys will be straight to work with, 'Aw, that's not fair' or 'What about Sue?'. A culture of consequences being fairly applied without fear or favour and with little room for negotiation gives boys the firm framework they need to work within.

Consequences also need to be applied without variation or emotional display and they especially need to be applied quickly. Watch boys playing computer games for prolonged periods. Boys who have had difficulty concentrating for periods in class or maintaining their focus for any length of time become most diligent and focused with a game in hand. It seems part of this is the immediacy of response: they make a mistake, they lose points or suffer the consequences; they win a competition, they are rewarded – immediately. No delay. No uncertainty that the consequence might be applied, or might not. Certainty of response and immediacy of response are most important for these boys.

Consequences need to be clearly explained so there is less chance of 'I didn't know I . . . ' or 'I thought I had until . . . '. There are always going to be students who willingly misinterpret and those who just do not listen. Boys are not good listeners, so clearly understood consequences determined early in the year, reinforced regularly and clearly explained each time they are imposed reduces ambiguity.

When rules are established at the start of the year there will follow a testing time.

Some boys will want to establish whether the rule is serious, and whether the teacher is serious about its enforcement. Things might get worse before they get better.

Those old enough to remember when it became compulsory to wear seatbelts in cars will remember that at the time many thought this was an infringement of personal choice. Continued police enforcement and advertising encouraged drivers to wear seatbelts. Gradually, the road toll was reduced, and now most people do not think twice before 'clicking and clacking'. In classes there will also be a time of resisting or testing, but hopefully less prolonged and with fewer casualties.

Ginger Meggs © Jimera P/L and Kemsley

Implementation of consequences

When implementing consequences, remember to keep the following in mind:

- Be consistent
- Be calm
- Be firm and unambiguous
- Do not be over-protective
- Allow a lag time
- Set a follow-up schedule

Consequences

Consider the following:
- What is the behaviour achieving?
- Does the student understand that the behaviour is inappropriate?
- Does the student understand what is appropriate?
- Is the student involved in determining the consequence?
- Is the consequence appropriate?
- Does the student understand the consequence?
- Does the student have a choice?
- Does the student understand why the consequence is being imposed?
- Is the consequence enforceable?
- Is the consequence immediate?

Figure 2.3   Examples of rules and consequences

Rule	Negative consequence
Be quiet in class	• complete work in own time • sit alone
Raise hand to talk	• ignored • rule reminder
Complete assigned work	• marking delayed • completion of work in own time
Work in a group	• loss of group marks • change of group
Listening when others are talking	• ignored • explaining to teacher in their own time what the problem was
Complete homework	• loss of marks • homework completed while class enjoys another activity
Keep hands to self	• isolation within class • removal from class (if appropriate)
Care for equipment	• exclusion from participation • do activity in own time
Arrive at class on time	• explain lateness after lesson • make up lost time • miss out on equipment use

My class rules

Rule	Negative consequences

Use the form below to list positive and negative consequences in hierarchical order.

Hierarchy of classroom consequences

Students	
Positive	**Negative**

Classroom teacher	
Positive	**Negative**

Executive (Head teacher/H.O.D./E.T./A.P./D.P./Coordinator)	
Positive	**Negative**

Figure 2.4   Integrating Behaviour

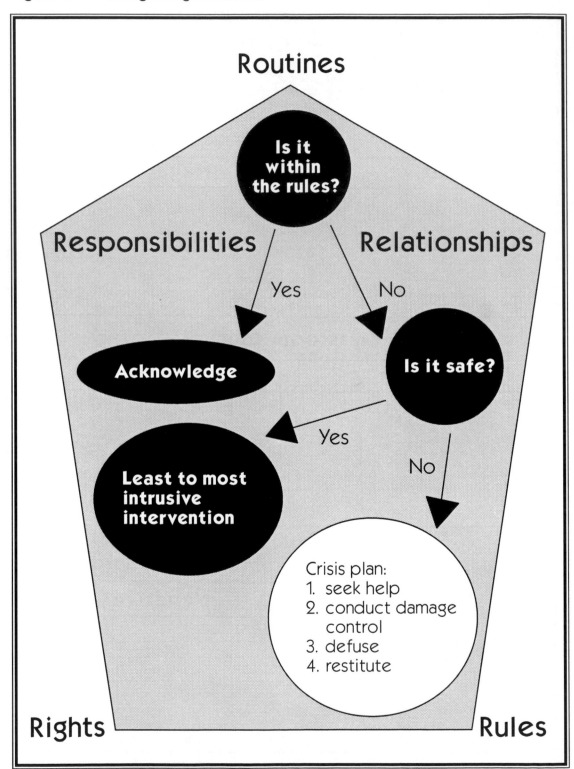

Competition

How many times has a group of boys who would not run out of sight on a dark night if they were instructed to do so gone on to flail themselves madly to 'beat the other team' when their instructor has made the run a competition? Boys especially like to compete, testing their skills and abilities against others, a set performance, or their own benchmarks.

Males compete, and good competition is far better than uneven affairs. Boys thrive on it. Playground conversations are regularly interrupted by confrontations along the lines of 'bet you can't' and 'bet I can'. It's an important part of their everyday interaction.

In classrooms there has been a move in recent years away from competition and towards cooperation. In some ways this has taken a driving force from many students, but especially boys. Reinforcing competition in the classroom does not mean ranking all students, displaying test scores or any of the many practices of the past that encouraged the reduction of competition from classrooms. Low-key competition in tasks that are within the scope of the students, with an accolade on reaching a set goal or reaching criteria is often all that is required. Recognition of the effort and participation in competitive struggle can help to build relationships with boys as they achieve.

The following points do not need to be a major part of the lesson, but they can be useful starter tools. The first moments of any lesson are crucial. If students don't arrive together or are not settled quickly there may be difficult moments in the offing. Boys do not want to sit and listen to drawn-out explanations at the start of the lesson, they want to get on with the job. So a small competition at the start of the lesson, maybe unrelated to the topic but short and a bit of fun and well within their abilities, might assist in establishing routines and the beginning of lessons. A short, fun problem on the board (not from the curriculum), when they start arriving, with a small reward for the first five finished, can be useful. For example, using the numbers 1, 2, 4, 6, 9, have students come up with a problem that equals 137. Students can multiply, add, divide or subtract the five digits to reach the final number. Answers are only taken from students with their books and pens out and ready. Alternatively, do a match puzzle or make ten words from the letters of 'English'. The puzzles should:

- not be too long (otherwise they eat into lesson time)
- not be too difficult (if students can't do them they won't participate)
- be done individually (no need to wait for a partner)
- focus attention on the board (to get students used to it)

- be completed in their seats (that's where students should be)

- be fun

This is just using competition to achieve the goal of having the students ready for the lesson.[1] Once the puzzle has been completed the lesson begins straight away, with students already seated and focused.

Competing against the teacher, finding all the words for a cloze passage, accurately reading a set of words quicker than their previous best time, getting their tables correct, spelling words both forwards and backwards, regular revision competitions between groups, measurement exercises – many small tasks can be made into stimulating activities for the boys through a little competition.

Conversely, displays and overt records can be a problem. In many primary and infant classes, star charts – charts drawn up with students' names down one side and spaces next to them for the 'stars' or stickers they achieve as they reach a goal – are used. Those students adept at following classroom rules or who can attract positive attention have lots of stars, while those students not so skilled have fewer. The achievement of successful students is demonstrated and reinforces their 'good' behaviour; however, it also reinforces inadequacies for others. All too often Susan, Mary, Katrina and Ann have long lines of stickers while Ben, John and Tom do not. These charts are not meant as competitions, but for boys trailing the field there can be bit of an edge. In those rooms where star charts are used, a simple reorganisation can be effective.

Circular charts can be useful (see page 73). Each student has an icon (a laminated symbol with a bit of blutack on the back) rather than a name and row. If students receive a negotiated reward after ten stars, rather than placing ten stars in a row, they could move their icon ten spaces on the chart. Rather than having a row of stars, the icon moves around a circular race achieving a reward every ten spaces. The students whose names were previously beside a large bright row of stars now move around the race quite quickly. Those students that previously had a long row of blanks now move around more slowly. But their relative speed around the race is not demonstrated for everyone. If all negotiated reward markers are equidistant from each other, then students do not have to all start at the same point on the chart but can be placed at many different points to avoid congestion and awareness of reward accumulation.

In some classes a single large chart might not be warranted. Smaller charts around the room might more adequately cater for individuals, groups or subject content. Changing the graphics on the chart periodically gives students the chance for a 'new start', raises interest as its appearance changes or allows the chart to be relevant to the topics being studied at the time.

Quick-and-easy lesson starters

1. Arrive at 179 using any combination of 9, 8, 6, 3, 1.

   For example,   9 x 6 = 54

   54 x 3 = 162

   162 + 8 = 170

   170 + 9 = 179

2. A boat with a rope ladder over the side is anchored in a harbour. Each rung of the ladder is half a metre apart. Water covers the bottom rung. If the tide is coming in at 1 metre per hour, how many rungs will be covered in 2 hours? (*Answer:* Only the bottom rung, as the boat floats up on the tide.)

3. Use this match puzzle to complete the problems below.

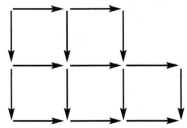

   a. Remove 2 matches and leave 3 boxes.   e. Move 2 matches and leave 4 boxes.

   b. Remove 3 matches and leave 3 boxes.   f. Move 3 matches and leave 4 boxes.

   c. Remove 4 matches and leave 3 boxes.   g. Move 4 matches and leave 4 boxes.

   d. Remove 5 matches and leave 3 boxes.   h. Move 5 matches and leave 5 boxes.

4. Make ten words of three or more letters from the letters of 'geography'.

   (*Answers:* graph, gear, gape, gore, grape, grope, gray, rage, rape, rope, reap, pear, pare, page, hare, hear, harp, rap, rag, ray, gap, gay, par, peg, year, hog, hay.)

5. Magic cubes

a	b	c	17
d	e	f	12
g	h	i	16

16   15   11

Perhaps a clue:

e = 7

c = 2

6. A fox, chicken and bag of wheat are on a river bank. A farmer wishes to move all three across the river, but if he leaves the chicken with the fox it will be eaten, as will the wheat if left with the chicken. His boat only holds one item at a time (as well as the farmer). Can he do it?

7. A farmer has cattle, wheat, sheep, goats and his home to fence separately. He can only build three fences and they must not cut across each other. Can he do it?

Ginger Meggs © Jimera P/L and Kemsley

A circular chart

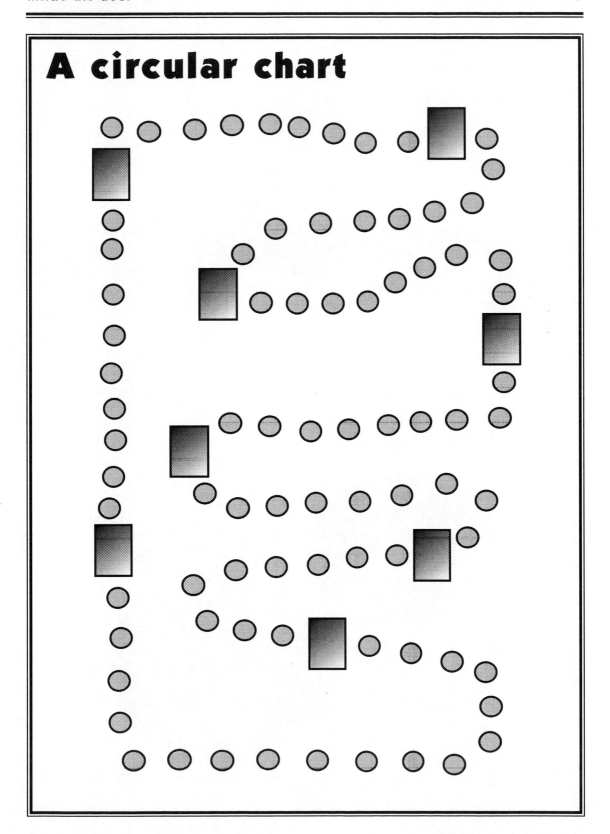

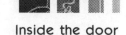

Figure 2.5   Each aspect considered

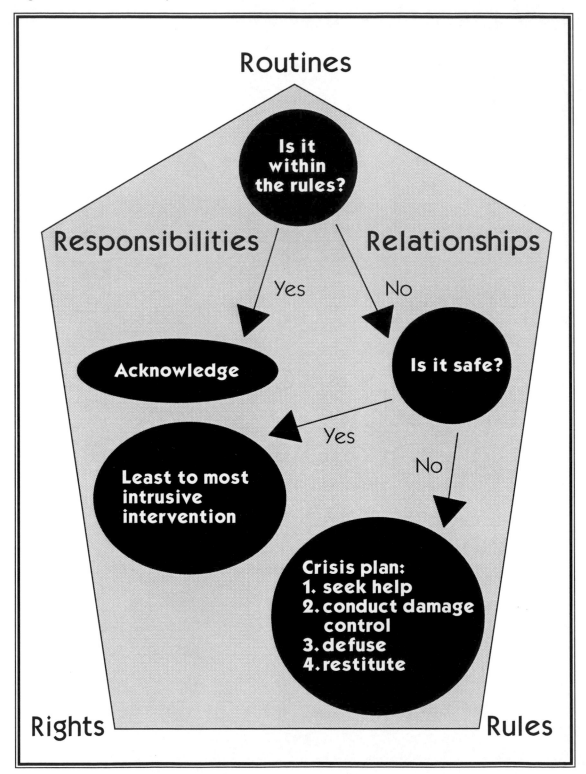

Talking and listening

Most teachers have been in the situation where they have painstakingly explained a process or situation for the class, gone over it, kept their voice modulated, used different expressions in the explanation and, feeling that all is well, have instructed the class to proceed only to be immediately asked, 'What are we supposed to be doin'?'. Whether in lower primary or post-compulsory secondary, an overwhelming desire to wreak havoc with the individual who asks that question is not uncommon. All too often the question is from the back or sides of the room and the questioner is male. All too often the teacher has noticed the boy during the explanation paying little attention to the instructions. All too often the student has drowned in the 'sea of blah'.

Ginger Meggs © Jimera P/L and Kemsley

Boys are not good listeners. Some commentators have suggested that the brains of males and females are different[2] and are wired differently. This results in different capabilities and characteristics. Some of these are important in classrooms, such as listening. Every family probably has stories about driving (with Dad at the wheel – as always) and some family conversations. Mum is able to talk and drive with the radio on or the window open, but Dad has to turn the radio off to take part in the conversation and probably winds the window up as well.

Girls' ability to perform multiple tasks is demonstrated throughout society. Family gatherings where the females engage in multiple conversations simultaneously on different topics while the males have difficulty coping with one conversation amidst the din are not too far removed from the classroom when Mary in the third row chats to her neighbour while the teacher is giving instructions, yet understands each point that has been made – in both conversations.

High school teachers faced with boys moving through adolescence may also suggest that these characteristics are exacerbated during this period, and that it does not assist them to sit and listen to academic discussion. In this period when their bodies are rapidly changing to cope with adulthood, and hormones are coursing their veins in bucketloads, sex seems rather more interesting than differential calculus, and for many

concentration on the single train of scholastic thought is difficult.

Ginger Meggs © Jimera P/L and Kemsley

Restless in themselves as they question their identity and the roles of those around them they relegate schoolwork to a lower priority. It has been suggested that adolescent boys think about sex on average 160 times a day. If eight hours are removed for sleeping, that comes in at about ten times per hour for the remainder of the day, or once every six minutes. It probably puts a whole new light on geology.

Attention Deficit Disorder and Attention Deficit Hyperactive Disorder also affect talking and listening. They are more regularly diagnosed in boys than girls – as are many other disorders – and reduce effective communication and, too often, learning. For these pupils there are additional barriers and a teacher's communication in the classroom needs to be especially efficient. The steps mentioned here will assist with some ADD or ADHD students, though they are not meant as a replacement for a properly developed learning plan.

With an assortment of media catering to shorter attention spans as a result of more commercials, short news articles, and scenes changing regularly in series produced for younger people, our classroom instructions also have to be short and sharp. Penetrating this maze and gaining students' attention may not be an easy or short-term task. Many have written about the 'sea of blah' – the instructions and talk given from the front of the room as students arrive to inform them of the desired outcome for the lesson, followed by a seemingly endless stream of verbiage. Boys especially drown in it.

Instructions

Instructions need to be given in short, direct chunks, and be quick and easy to follow. Long sentences or instructions that seem interminable only accelerate the downward spiral, but short and sharp instructions and direct words in short sentences get boys moving.

Consider the following instructions:

- Read Chapter 3 before recess.
- Read Chapter 3 before recess, will you?
- Would you read Chapter 3 before recess, please?
- Do you think we should read Chapter 3 before recess?
- Wouldn't it be good if we read Chapter 3 before recess?
- Do you feel like reading Chapter 3 before recess?

The first three are more direct, and represent the kind of instructions to which boys seem to react more favourably. The latter three are less direct and these seem to create more problems for boys than girls. Boys might have difficulty understanding that Chapter 3 is to be read before going to recess when they are offered options unrelated to the task.

Instructions should be given using multimedia. This may comprise verbal instructions complemented by a written outline, so that all can see where they are going. Verbal instruction should be repeated as standard – if it hasn't been said three times it hasn't been said. Even after repetition, some will, with the best of intentions, forget where they are going, just what the process was, or how the steps were organised. Visually presented goals or instructions will assist some to check where they should be going if they need to.

When instructions have been adequately given to students, no questions should be answered for a short period. This might be twenty seconds. With some classes it might be a bit longer or shorter. This is to encourage students to listen when instructions are given but also to examine their peers' actions before asking questions. Many of those disruptive questions asked immediately after finishing outlining an activity can be removed if students *know* their question will not be answered, and can train themselves to observe their classmates. Some students are a little slower at processing verbally given information and some will seek separate instruction. The time lag will encourage them to observe before querying. Some students have been doing just this for a long time: students with hearing impairments are usually quite adept at working out what they are meant to be doing by observing their cohort's reaction to instructions.

Organisation

Boys are not the best organisers. Whether it be time, how to present material or how much effort is required for each section, boys often need to organise more for longer tasks.

Lessons may need to be organised into chunks that boys will see that they can attempt. If the lesson instructions, whether verbal or nonverbal, are too long or complicated,

many will shut off. Not only do the instructions need to be given in short format but the lesson also needs to be seen as achievable. A long list of tasks, giving the impression that they will be in until next week, will not entice participation.

Prompts

Individual prompts can also be useful. These are small cards with the steps of the process or skill used in the lesson outlined and placed on the desk of students who may need reminding. Then, as the lesson proceeds, students can, if necessary, be redirected by simply moving past their desk and drawing their attention to the prompts, usually in a non-confrontational manner designed to not draw attention from others in the class.

Examples of prompts

Across before up
Find north
1 cm = 10 mm

Add and subtract left to right
Divide before multiply
Brackets first

1. Read a paragraph.
2. Pick out the key words.
3. Underline the main sentence.
4. Make 1–2 points.

Use the questions below to assess talking and listening in your classroom.

Teacher location

In each lesson, how much teacher time is spent

- at the teacher's desk?

| 0% | 10% | 20% | 30% | 40% | 50% | 60% | 70% | 80% | 90% | 100% |

- at the front centre of the room?

| 0% | 10% | 20% | 30% | 40% | 50% | 60% | 70% | 80% | 90% | 100% |

- giving instructions to the whole student body?

| 0% | 10% | 20% | 30% | 40% | 50% | 60% | 70% | 80% | 90% | 100% |

- reinforcing instructions to individual students?

| 0% | 10% | 20% | 30% | 40% | 50% | 60% | 70% | 80% | 90% | 100% |

- redirecting students once the task has been begun?

| 0% | 10% | 20% | 30% | 40% | 50% | 60% | 70% | 80% | 90% | 100% |

- out of students' eyesight?

| 0% | 10% | 20% | 30% | 40% | 50% | 60% | 70% | 80% | 90% | 100% |

- affirming student performance?

| 0% | 10% | 20% | 30% | 40% | 50% | 60% | 70% | 80% | 90% | 100% |

- giving feedback on how students are performing?

| 0% | 10% | 20% | 30% | 40% | 50% | 60% | 70% | 80% | 90% | 100% |

- reinforcing class rules?

| 0% | 10% | 20% | 30% | 40% | 50% | 60% | 70% | 80% | 90% | 100% |

- applying consequences for rule breakages?

| 0% | 10% | 20% | 30% | 40% | 50% | 60% | 70% | 80% | 90% | 100% |

- collecting material/completed tasks/homework?

| 0% | 10% | 20% | 30% | 40% | 50% | 60% | 70% | 80% | 90% | 100 |

Figure 2.6   Bringing the group together

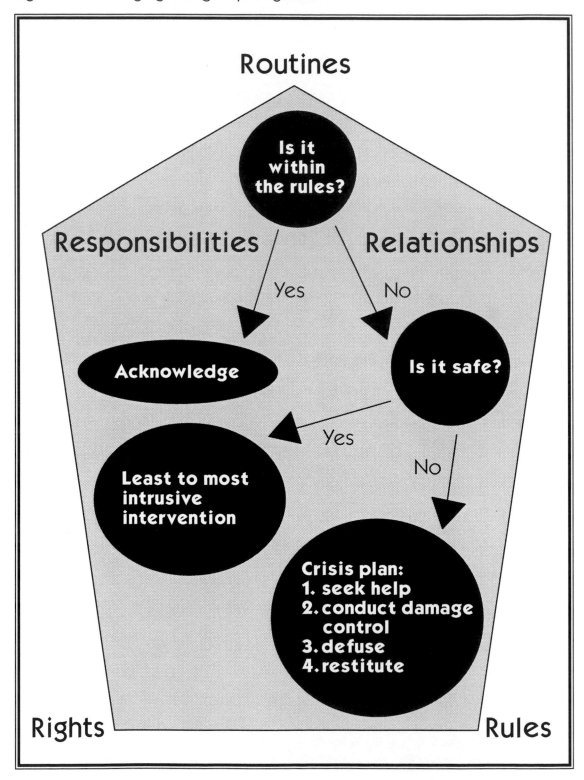

Group work

For many boys, group work means 'how to get the most marks for the least effort' or 'how to get someone else to do the work'. Many boys prefer to work alone rather than in groups, while girls seem readily able to settle in to working together, discussing the project at hand, organising and cooperating. However, with some patience and organisation, all groups can participate without too much trauma, and the benefits of successful group work may be achieved. For all students, group work:

- caters for individual differences

- promotes cooperation, tolerance, helping and learning with others

- allows tasks to be broken into achievable steps that are allied to ability levels or skills

- encourages students to work independently of the teacher and thus at their own pace

- encourages students to assume responsibilities within the group and develop relationships as they work

- encourages peer tutoring and, by developing group identity, can encourage greater achievement, especially from the less motivated

- encourages students to appreciate perspectives of situations other than their own;

- allows a variety of activities to occur simultaneously

- provides opportunities for pro-social behaviour modification through peer interaction

Some of these are of particular relevance for boys, and some will present difficulties. Boys will determine their outcome, and for many the main aim will remain how to get the piece of work completed quickly and with the least effort. Therefore, teacher preparation should ensure that the completed piece of work is not the only outcome and is not the only assessment, and that all students know this.

The group size should be determined before the negotiating phase begins. Remember that the bigger the group the easier it is to hide and the easier it is to find someone else to complete the task or blame for not completing it. Variables when considering group size include:

- **Age** – younger students should work in smaller groups.

- **Previous experience** in group work. Less experienced students should work in smaller groups.

- **Resources or nature of the task** may dictate group size and number.

- **Time** – the larger the group, the more time students may need to complete a task. This may increase the chance of students not being able to concentrate or follow the path.

- **Complexity** – the longer the task, the more complex the instructions and the greater the chance of students not completing it – either by not following or by giving up. Boys will want to see a task that they can complete, so complex instructions may need to be broken up into chunks either for each period or on completion of the previous chunk.

- **Visual reminders** should complement verbal explanations of the task. These may include:
  - The purpose of the task
  - How it fits into the lesson sequence
  - Objectives – learning and others such as social skills
  - Outlines of task steps
  - Suggested time for each step and total time estimate

Group selection

Group selection seems to be on three bases. In the classroom there is often a microsecond between determining group size and beginning the process of selecting groups. But they are distinct.

Teacher selected

Groups decided through the teacher monitoring and selecting may be the best in terms of academic outcomes. Variation within groups as to who completes which tasks may relate to student experience, the culture of the classroom or the task at hand. Groups should be comparable but internally heterogeneous. Peer groups can either be split up or allowed to work together. Sexes can be mixed.

Student selected

Student-selected groups are determined by friendship, common interests or common abilities. Boys tend to choose to work with boys, as do the girls; more able students tend to choose their ilk. Groups may not be so comparable and are often not as internally heterogeneous. Non-academic outcomes may be more difficult to achieve, but students may be initially happier to be working with groups of their own choice.

Randomly selected

Numbers, dice, or names pulled out of a hat can be used to select groups randomly. This can be fun and when scrupulously done will produce random groups that may be used for comparison purposes. However, this method has neither the student support of working with their friends, nor teacher guidance, so groups might not be suitable.

Most students prefer to make their own decisions about whom they are going to be with, but many educators prefer heterogeneous groups where differences are highlighted. In randomly selected groups there are likely to be wider differences in

points of view, and greater giving and receiving of explanations and peer tutoring. On the down side, initial support might not be as strong as desired.

Group organisation

Group organisation can be important. If group work is to continue over a reasonable period of time, relationships may alter and students may have difficulty working with each other. Some options include:

Facing each other

Students working around tables pointing towards the centre facilitates good eye contact and has each student facing most of the group. This group structure will probably involve desk movement and restrictions on group size. There may be difficulties with students facing each other. If there are issues between group members, facing each other can be difficult, and for boys it may not lead to effective work being undertaken. The formation seems to work well for girls who readily and easily discuss their work with several people.

Close together

If students do not need to work together but can work separately or in subgroups and bring their work together at various points, they may be able to sit near each other without having to work at the same table. Students will want to communicate with other group members and there may be additional movement as a result. Pairs or subgroups can work independently, so the grouping arrangements can be ameliorated. There is a need for the social aims of the group work to be kept in mind. Under this arrangement group discussion may be difficult, although seating arrangements need minimal changes. Boys may well prefer this alternative as they are able to work in smaller subgroups or individually, avoiding the social skill aims.

Relative to materials

Groups organised relative to materials may need to rotate periodically. There may be restrictions on time with different resources that may not suit students working at different paces. This can be useful when there are insufficient resources for all groups or when the social skill objective is related to this aspect. That the resources vary may encourages boys to complete sections and move on to the next 'adventure', but excessive movement will be unsettling, and if work is not completed from one resource group to the next, there will be concern.

Within groups girls are more able to organise tasks and their time than boys. Boys may well divide work along lines of their pecking order, coercion and work avoidance rather than assessment of tasks and relative skills of group members. Some definition of roles or group structures may reduce unfair allocations and develop skills of group members.

Jigsaw materials

Here each member is given some material, but not enough to complete the entire task. Boys can work in their preferred style for some of the time and compile the group presentation as they complete sections.

Sharing one set of materials

Here each group is given one set of materials. All members use the same resources at the same time to compile either individual or group presentations. Within the group, interactions vary allowing peer tutoring or individual work. Without internal structure there can be task avoidance and inappropriate distribution.

Assigning roles

Roles assigned may include recorder, reporter, timekeeper, checker, summariser, observer, noise monitor. Each role is defined and appointed for the duration of the task. Laminated role cards can assist recognition and reminders of roles.

Group assessment

Assessment of group work without rewarding some who have not fully participated or penalising those who may have performed additional tasks to cover under-performers is always difficult. In the long-term, peer assessment can be a useful tool. If the finished product is able to be reviewed by the rest of the class, preferably without group names observable but ordered in an anonymous manner (such as using numbers or letters), pairing class members and giving each pair the criteria upon which the finished product is to be assessed allows class members a review process for their own work. It enables them to observe aspects of others' work that may be appealing and aspects that may or may not address the criteria. Signing the marking sheet identifies the markers, and this may be a part of the assessment process in itself.

Other useful methods include:

- Selecting a student from each group to demonstrate or explain the group position and understanding at any time during the process.
- Randomly selecting a work sheet from a group's presentation. This will encourage all members to have responsibility for the quality of the final product.
- Using a group process chart to find the average of each group's performance as the process continues.
- Peer assessment, with each group assessing their own product with guidelines prepared by the teacher. The remainder of the class also assesses other groups' work.

Group activity assessment

Topic _____   Time _____

	Choice	Reason
Group size		
Selection method		
Group organisation		
Group structure		

Academic evaluation

_____
_____
_____

Social evaluation

_____
_____
_____

Things to do differently next time:

_____
_____
_____

The teacher

As teachers move around the room they can spot students off task and assist them with low-key interventions. This makes difficult for students to be sure of the teacher's location. Sedentary staff or those using only a small portion of the room from which to supervise a lesson give students every opportunity to be sure of the teacher's location. If teachers are moving about the room, spending some time out of eyesight for some students, moving behind students who have work to carry on with, then the 'teacher radar' is not as effective. Off-task activities might be engaged in, or there will be head movement similar to a periscope in a calm pond which will attract teacher attention and can be quickly addressed before the behaviour escalates.

For many boys, the sight of a staff member approaching them directly raises apprehension and fears that they might have transgressed in some manner, and, as the adrenalin begins to flow, 'fight or flight' mechanisms cut in. For many adolescent boys in front of their peers, 'flight' in this situation is not an option. If there is to be difficulty in class, the boy in question will be is preparing before the teacher has begun speaking. Every teacher has moved towards a boy at some stage, in their full vision, and before the teacher can begin speaking is asked, 'What've I done?', usually in a tone not reserved for social niceties. Approaching from the side or behind, reducing the period of apprehension and build-up as the student watches a staff member approaching, can reduce some of these instances. If the teacher is wandering the room, out of sight for short periods, his or her appearance at the elbow or near a boy to enquire how he is going is not so confronting – especially when this is the regular pattern in the classroom.

When doing this, as in most interventions with students, the focus of the enquiry should be the task rather than the behaviour that has attracted attention. Saying to a student, 'What are you talking about?', 'Why were you talking?' or 'Stop talking' invites responses such as:

- I wasn't talking

- It's none of your business

- What do you mean . . . talking?

- I wasn't talking. I only said . . .

- Why are you picking on me? Mary was . . .

The list is endless. The attention of the class is on the entertainment created. The focus of the students is now on the behaviour rather than on their lesson. By focusing on their task rather than on the behaviour and asking questions like, 'How are you going with question 5?' disrupts their conversation, focuses them on the task and is not

confrontational. Boys especially have a single focus. If we direct the focus to the behaviour, then it is harder to get many boys back on task. If teachers focus on the task, the behaviour is more easily removed. Responses to this intervention might be:

- This sux
- I'm having difficulty with question 2
- I've already finished question 8
- I'm up to question 4 and I'm discussing the answer to 5 with Bill

These responses are certainly less entertaining for the class and, while some are certainly not positive, they are generally related to the task and within the learning situation rather than the secondary behaviour cycle students are expert at discussing.

This method avoids a confrontational situation and the potential for the teacher to be perceived as criticising the student. For many boys, such criticism can be seen as a put-down, detracting from their position in the pecking order. If they are already considerably disengaged from their schooling and disenchanted with learning, then retaliation is a win–win situation for them. 'Standing up the teacher' wins kudos for some and reduces the learning opportunities for many. Focusing on the task does not ignore the behaviour. That is why the student has been asked the question, has the teacher's proximity and is being refocused onto the task to achieve the goal without confrontation.

If some discussion about the behaviour is warranted, then preferably a private conversation without the student's peers in the corridor or after the lesson might be appropriate. For many boys public remonstration only fuels the fire of angst and disengagement. Before his mates many an adolescent boy will have difficulty accepting a rebuke from staff unless they are well respected. 'Fight' could well be the mode of operation.

Just as discipline matters might be best discussed in private, so too might praise. Many of the boys in classes find it difficult to accept public praise for their work. Before their peers it may not be terribly cool to gain accolades, and positive reinforcement might have a negative impact. This probably needs to be ascertained and the culture attacked over a period of time, but in the short-term personal positive reinforcement might also need to be private.

At each point of intervention teachers should remain calm. Many boys will react to those teachers who readily demonstrate anger and frustration. In general, boys need to:

- know the rules
- know that they are being dealt with fairly

- maintain their own position in the class hierarchy
- know who is in charge

If the nominal leader – the teacher – exhibits actions that are not good leadership, then boys will become stressed. For many boys, anger and frustration are emotions that they are familiar with, and they will have done their homework on how they are going to react. Consider the following:

- Power players raise their own hackles, and confrontation with staff can be the outcome.

- Revenge seekers accept the display of anger or frustration but take offence and either withdraw or seek revenge later.

- Attention seekers see this as an opportunity to gain peer and teacher attention. It may lead to competition as to who can achieve the 'best' teacher reaction.

And for those who feel inadequate, the expression of frustration or anger just reinforces inadequacy.[3]

Good teaching

Research is showing that boys in particular respond to teachers who know the curriculum. Recent research from Suffolk regarding senior primary students' literacy has teacher knowledge of texts as the first prerequisite of what works for boys, with a following suggestion that senior teachers be responsible for literacy in Year 5 and 6 to give it kudos.[4] The work of Slade and Trent at Flinders University[5] reinforces this, as does the practice in many schools where senior teachers are placed on senior classes.

A point to have in the back of every teacher's mind is the repeated comment by boys in surveys such as the one above that they respond to interest and enthusiasm. If teaching staff are not demonstrating the enthusiasm that encouraged them to initially apply for their positions, in the words of one:

The teacher was not going to teach, so we decided not to learn.[6]

Good teaching will assist all students. Rowe suggests that once systemic and school variation are accounted for, teaching is responsible for over half of the variation in student outcomes.[7] Just what good teaching translates into varies from classroom to classroom. Maintaining an interesting, challenging, positive learning environment while addressing the cultural, socioeconomic and day-to-day variations of a group of students is in itself interesting. To find that piece of the puzzle enabling students to succeed above the norm is rewarding for all.

Teachers might use the space below to write their own ideas about what makes good teaching. If there is not enough space, use blank paper.

Notes

I believe

_____

_____

_____

I encourage

_____

_____

_____

I allow

_____

_____

_____

I limit

_____

_____

_____

As class time progresses there will be students who need more structure. A simple structure that reinforces classroom processes without intruding into established routines is the 'three strikes' formula. Perhaps not having quite as severe an impact as Northern Territory legislation, it lets some boys know that they are moving along the continuum, rather than finding out when the teacher explodes and removes them from the room without – in their mind – giving them warning. Most executive teachers and behaviour specialists will have discussed tactics with students who have bemoaned, 'Everything was fine, and then Sir/Miss sent me out'. Some of these complaints demonstrate that the student was not aware of the increasing severity of teacher intervention, while some may be reasonable.

Boys do not have a good track record at reading body language or voice tone. When they have not understood warning signals given to them by teachers – and quite probably other class members – that their actions are causing concern, they continue blissfully until the intervention level is sufficient to impinge on their senses. When this occurs, the boy is on occasion unsure, in front of his mates, with his position in the boys' pecking order in the balance. He won't go down without a bit of a fight. The three strikes process lets them know that they are moving along the continuum and just where they are up to in the process.

Things to think about

How do you:

- inform students of class expectations and the reasons for them?

- find out students' expectations and use them to shape the classroom?

- build on students' life experiences in your teaching?

- ensure there is consistency among subject objectives, pedagogy and assessment?

- create opportunities for students to focus on preferred aspects of the course?

- extend your teaching practices to cater for varying learning styles or needs?

- indicate that you respect students' values without accepting them?

- encourage students to learn from one another?

- show enthusiasm for your subject?

- make a conscious effort to be a role model?

- frame questions to help students learn effectively?

- encourage questions from students?

- check that your answers are understood?

cont.

- respond when students indicate difficulty with course content or pace?

- investigate disruptive behaviour?

- use information from tests or assignments to evaluate your teaching?

- keep your expertise up-to-date?

How often do you:

- discuss aspects of teaching or learning with your colleagues?

- encourage feedback on your teaching from colleagues?

- reflect on your own teaching, identifying areas for improvement?

Figure 2.7   And you're out

Least intrusive

3 Strikes

Student is off-task

> Tactically ignore as appropriate
> Give clear, low-key intervention
> Create body proximity
> Focus on task
> Provide rule reminder
> FIRST WARNING

Focus on primary behaviour

Student continues off-task

> Repeat direction or question
> Verify student knows what to do
> Restate rule
> Redirect if appropriate
> Direct student aside as appropriate
> SECOND WARNING

Focus on relevant rule/right

Student continues off-task

> Give choice with known consequence
> Direct student away from peers
> THIRD WARNING

Focus on process not personality

Student continues off-task

> Exit from classroom

Re-establish working relationship with student

Most intrusive

Notes

1. Additionally, students may try to arrive earlier to class to get a bit more time at the puzzle and thus more chance for a reward. It can be nice when other teachers notice that students are making an effort to be at your lesson early.

2. Anne Moir & David Jessel, *Brainsex*, Mandarin, 1989, and Anne & Bill Moir, *Why men don't iron*, Harper Collins, London, 1998.

3. Dreikurs, Grunwald & Pepper, *Maintaining sanity in the classroom*, Harper & Row, 1982.

4. Sally Rundell, 'Suffolk study into what works for boys and writing', TES, June 2001.

5. 'Listening to the boys' in *Boys in schools journal*, vol. 4, no. 1, pp. 10–18.

6. 2JJJ phone interview, February 2001.

7. Dr K. Rowe, 'Equal and different? Yes but what really matters?' Background paper to keynote address presented at the joint conference of The Alliance of Girls' Schools (Australasia) and The International Boys' Schools Coalition (Australian Hub), Southport School, Queensland, 3–5 August 2001.

part 3

Crisis

Figure 3.1   The crisis plan

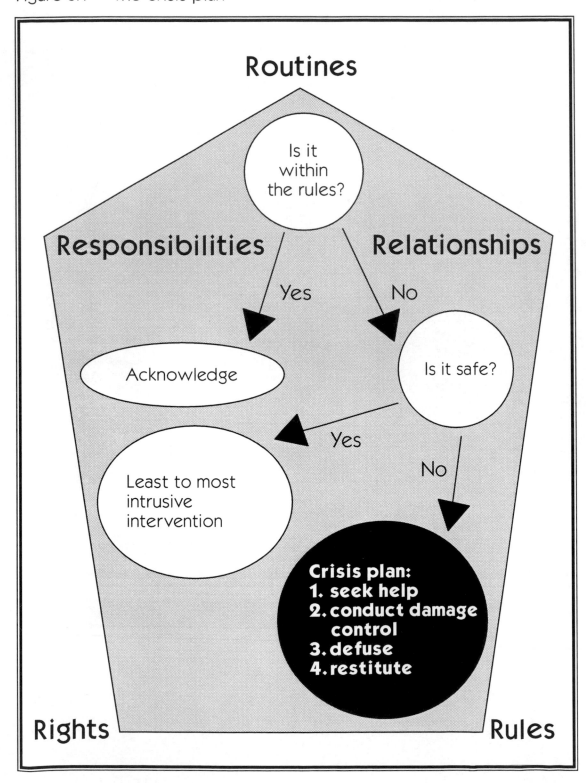

Techniques for the special student

Following is a list of things to consider for the special student.

- Provide activities at their own level.

- Provide distractions through jobs, activities, etc.

- Provide conditioning

- Allow the distressed student to move from the potentially difficult situation and:

  - write a message

  - get a drink

  - run in the playground

  - see the counsellor

  - sit in a quiet place

  - provide peer support

- Give the student outlets for angry feelings through physical activities such as art, craft, sport, drama, using a punching bag.

- Explain to students, on their own, why specific things happen.

- Establish with students that they make choices regarding their behaviour and that this is their responsibility.

- It is important that consequences for inappropriate behaviour are established and that students know they will be applied. The certainty of a consequence is more of a deterrent than the consequence itself.

- Establish a warm, trusting relationship.

- Provide clearly defined time-out facilities, and:

  - Explain what time-out is.

  - Do not enter into lengthy explanations about the whys and wherefores.

  - Allow sufficient cooling-off time.

  - Reduce anxiety.

  - Be specific about length of stay.

- Keep a record of behaviour to:

  - outline goals.

  - measure progress

- – praise and encourage effort

- – report progress as appropriate

- Have the students monitor their own behaviour.

- Have ready access to student progress card/records.

- Encourage acceptance of a particular student by the class. Reward the student's group for their cooperation then reward the class similarly.

- Avoid techniques which have failed either at home or for other staff.

- Use the student's imagination in a positive way using:

  - – relaxation

  - – games

  - – visual imagery

  - – role-playing

  - – miming

  - – fantasy

Crisis

Thirty years ago teachers could focus much of their time on the learning of students. Unfortunately, our society has added many other responsibilities over the intervening years, while insisting the quality of education be at least maintained. Along with these changes has been an increase in violence.

An increase in violence in society has been well documented and now the increase within schools is attracting attention. Teachers should prepare for instances of violence and plan their method of response. Buddies, teams, stages or groups of staff together should prepare for a crisis to present a considered and reasonable response that quickly and effectively restores the situation to normal.

Following is a selection of news headlines from various papers relating to schools and some of the issues confronted by staff.

Newspaper headlines

Janitor's find foils school shooting plot – The Daily Telegraph, *28 November 2001*

$2.2m to calm gang violence – The Daily Telegraph, *11 July 2001*

Drink problems hurting 1 in 10 younger people – The Sydney Morning Herald, *8 September 1998*

Laughter canned in miserable 90's – Herald Sun, *1 November 1998*

Parents told they can help stop violence – The Sunday Telegraph, *16 April 2000*

Youth suicide on the rise – the experts speculate why – The Sydney Morning Herald, *2 August 2001*

Special schools for rowdy kids – Herald Sun, *17 June 2001*

State hides school discipline crisis – The Courier Mail, *1 March 2000*

Migrants' children beat boys in literacy – The Sydney Morning Herald, *1 May 2000*

Bullied with nowhere to turn – The Sunday Telegraph, *16 April 2000*

Death of five 'good blokes' stuns town – The Daily Telegraph, *29 January 2001*

Schools of violence – teachers forced to take AVOs against pupils – The Sunday Telegraph, *19 August 2001*

Boys take the honours – in wagging – The Sydney Morning Herald, *7 June 2001*

Boy suspended over toy gun – The Daily Telegraph, *3 July 2001*

Most often, violence is a tool of boys. Juvenile and adult incarceration figures for violence are heavily weighted against girls, with fraud being the only category where the sexes are not disproportionately weighted.[1] The trend in schools is similar, as demonstrated by suspension rates, with teachers expected to cope with outbursts that are quite foreign to many and are not part of their training. Situations can arise from seemingly minor events in the classroom, corridors, playgrounds or moving to and from excursions, sport and school. Perpetrators may be school students, community members, parents or siblings. Preparation for crises has to account for myriad factors outside the control, and probably the awareness, of teachers. Local issues will affect responses and the type of support that can be expected.

Below are some general points regarding any crisis situation that can be used as a guide.

Listen positively

Some crises can be avoided by lending an ear. The boy is frustrated, no-one wants to hear 'his side', he is 'fed up' and has reached the point where he can no longer keep his frustration and anger bottled up. He feels he needs to let it out. This might be physical, but an empathic listener may reduce these occurrences. Encouraging the boy to vent his anger and frustration verbally can reduce the need for physical release. Some boys will not be able to freely express themselves and positive listening skills may be needed to encourage him.

Clarify what is said

Check that he is saying what he means. Under pressure, many people will say many things that later, when they are calm, they readily acknowledge that they did not really mean. It is important to agree, ask questions, confirm that it is okay to be angry (but not to hit people as a result), make sure that he has every opportunity to vent his anger, express himself and tell his story.

Avoid overreacting

Some students' stories are outside the scope and experience of teachers, but are quite 'normal' for the student, and if the opportunity is to be taken to assist, reacting unsupportively to information will reduce the chance of success. Reaction is often akin to judgment.

Overreaction has another facet in crises that have gone beyond the verbal. Calmness is an attribute that when projected in crisis situations increases the chances of success. Whether it be responding to injuries, confronting an aggressive person, or breaking up a melee, projecting calmness can only assist.

Keep personal space

Respecting personal space of distraught or upset people, as well as ensuring your own, reduces perceived threatening positions and increases teacher safety.

Non-threatening non-verbals

Keeping side-on is less threatening and reduces your target areas. Keeping your hands in sight reduces the chance of a distraught mind concluding that a weapon is being prepared. (It also means your hands are out and ready for defence.) Keep a clearway between the distraught person and an exit. Eye contact needs to empathic.

Allow venting

For some, verbal release of pent-up emotions will involve expressions, often loud, that are not usually used at the dinner table. If anger can be released in this manner it can be preferable to physical release.

Set reasonable limits

Most crisis situations need to have a conclusion, and be contained where possible. Behaviours need to be curtailed where possible to reduce escalation. Rigidly enforcing limits that are too restrictive is counterproductive while too lax a position might incite further action.

Only get physical as a last resort

Talking a crisis through is the best option for all parties. Physical restraint should only be used as a last resort.

Remove the audience

An audience heightens the situation and will reduce the chances of a student backing down. Removal, where possible, may reduce trauma for those watching.

Get assistance

Additional staff, specialists, support personnel and police can provide appropriate assistance. Trying to handle a situation on your own, when support is available, is fraught with danger.

Ignore challenges

Challenges are like secondary behaviours. Upset boys may try to personify their issues and a close target is easiest. When they are having difficulty with their emotions an immediate solution may be preferred.

Confrontation

If there is a fight, and the crowd around is pushing contestants back into the centre, if one is less keen than the other, do the following:

* Get assistance – better two heads than one
* Remove the audience – reduces the fun
* Verbal first – talk first, act later
* Physical last – don't step between them
* Use a distraction – once the fight is over
* Separate – out of sight, out of mind

Weapons are banned from all schools, although sometimes they are sighted and used, with disastrous effects. Without dwelling on the repercussions of weapons in schools, some general points to keep in mind include:

Stay calm if possible. Most probably the student is not calm, but if the weapon has not been used yet then there is not a certainty that it will be used at all. However, if involved staff are not calm, it will most likely exacerbate the situation and potential use may become actual use.

Focus on the student, not the weapon. Most weapons will not hurt anyone unless they are manipulated by someone. Try to focus on the student or person holding the weapon. This person is probably excited, upset and unsure.

Negotiate and try to get agreement on something. Question like, 'Is it okay if I stand here?' are useful. The more agreement the less chance of the weapon being used. This is also buying time.

Personal space is important. If there can be a little space between the student and

yourself, it is less threatening to the student, and can help reduce their trauma. It might also reduce accuracy.

Buy time. The longer the student is kept talking the better the chance for help to arrive, for them to calm down and the less likely that the weapon will be used. Empathic listening, clarifying demands, checking any instructions might gain time.

Physical disarming is dangerous. Unless it is the *only* option, it is not an option.

These are general guidelines only and expert assistance is necessary to prepare teachers for violent situations. Each school has a management plan for serious incidents and staff should be familiar with its processes.

What can we do?

Following are some steps that in the longer term might reduce the chances of violence. They will not remove the chance of outbursts but, by establishing a learning environment that students are comfortable in, where the rules are known, and are enforced fairly and without personal angst by teachers who are recognised as knowledgeable, respected as fair and who care for the students, such incidents may be reduced in frequency and intensity.

Develop a relationship that the child values.

- Be constant and predictable.
- Accept the child not the behaviour.
- Show the child that they are worthwhile.
- Share jokes.
- Find opportunities to say positive things.
- Move away when the student cannot cope with having you around.

Change attitudes through constant discussion.

- Exploit opportunities to train.
- Interpret feeling back to the student ('You are feeling angry because . . . ').
- Listen and provide feedback to the student.
- Ensure students makes the decisions regarding their behaviour.

Change behaviour first.

- Set clear limits on behaviour.
- Respond calmly to severe outbursts.

- Try to change the behaviour of the group to which the student belongs.
- Role-play experiences.
- Expect compliance in small things first.
- Use repetition.
- Use emotional appeal.
- Try to get the student to identify with change.
- Reduce anxiety.

Develop all possible ego strengths.

- Enhance the student's awareness of body and appearance.
- Teach the student to use language effectively.
- Structure interests around the student's strengths.
- Use hobbies, skills, school work, social interaction.
- Provide opportunities for success wherever possible.

Give the students a chance to isolate themselves.

- Provide a safe place.
- Provide a time-out place.
- Allow choice in determining when they need to use these spaces.

Encourage peer group involvement.

- Reward the peer group for the student's effort.
- Reward the peer group for their effort.
- Encourage the peer group to support the student.

Constantly suggest change and recognise improvement.

- Have regular discussions with the student alone.
- Provide regular reinforcement for the student in the group.
- Regularly praise achievement.

Record improvement.

- Involve the student in recording.
- Give constant feedback.

Some suggested goals in class include students:

- staying in their seats

- putting their hands up without interrupting

- completing small tasks as requested

- listening carefully when others are speaking

- developing cooperative responses

- working as a team

- developing specific skills

Further reading

Armstrong, T., *Awakening genius*, ASCD, Alexandria, 1998.

Bosch, K., *Planning classroom management for change*, Hawker Brownlow Education, Melbourne, 2000.

Bozzone, M., 'Spend less time refereeing and more time teaching', *Instructor*, New York, vol. 104 no. 1, pp. 88–93, 1994.

Berman, S., *Making choice theory work in a quality classroom*, Hawker Brownlow Education, Melbourne, 1998.

Gilbert, P. & Gilbert, R., *Masculinity goes to school*, Allen & Unwin, Sydney, 1998.

Murphy, P. & Gipps, C., *Equity in the classroom*, Falmer, London, 1996.

Collins, C., Batten, M., Ainley, J. & Getty, C., *Gender & school education*, ACER, Melbourne, 1996.

Munn, P., Johnstone, M. & Chambers, V., *Effective discipline in primary school classrooms*, Chapman, London, 1992.

Gilbert, P. & Rowe, K., *Gender, literacy and the classroom*, Australian Reading Association, Melbourne, 1989

Moloney, J., *Boys and books*, ABC, Adelaide, 2001.

Notes

1. Australian Institute of Criminology: facts and figures, Canberra, 2000.

Bibliography

ACER, 'Educational disadvantage may need to be re-evaluated', media release, Melbourne, 14 February 2001.

Arndt, B., 'A better deal for boys', *The Sydney Morning Herald*, 29 May 2001, and *The Australian*, 24 March 2001, p. 13.

Australian Council for Educational Administration, *Directions in education*, Melbourne, vol. 10.

Australian Institute of Criminology, *Australian crime: facts and figures*, Canberra, 2000.

Baird, J., 'You're out: principals tell students', *The Sydney Morning Herald*, 1 June 2001.

Browne, R. & Fletcher, R., eds *Boys in schools*, Finch, Sydney, 1995.

Biddulph, S., *Raising boys*, Finch, Sydney, 1997.

Biddulph, S., Edgar D., Fletcher R., *Leadership in boys' education*, University of Newcastle, 1999.

Biernbaum, M., 'School safe: stopping violence without violence', *International journal of protective behaviours*, New York, vol. 1 no. 1, 1995.

Brown, M., *Image of a man*, East Publications, New York, 1976.

Campbell, D., 'Teachers to be insured for murder on the job', *The Sydney Morning Herald*, 28–29 July 2001.

Clarke P., 'I'll get you at lunch', *Boys in schools*, Browne, R. and Fletcher, R., eds, Finch, Sydney, 1995, pp. 168–177.

Cole, M., 'State hides school discipline crisis', *The Courier-Mail*, 1 March 2000.

Conoley, A., Goldstein P. & Close J., eds, *School violence intervention: a practical handbook*, Guildford, 1997.

Cook, M., 'Schools failing boys', *The Age*, 6 June 2001.

Glasser, W., *Control theory: a new explanation of how we control our lives*, Harper & Rowe, New York, 1984.

Gender and Equities in Education, Stanford, vol. 1, issue 1, 1998.

Grubb, J., 'Research briefing on boys and underachievement from the TES', University of Cambridge School of Education, United Kingdom, June 2001.

Herald Sun, The, 6 March 2001, p. 58.

Holborow, B., Kids: *loving for life*, Random House, Sydney, 1999.

Ireland, P., 'Nurturing boys, developing skills', *Boys in schools*, Browne, R. & Fletcher, R., eds, Finch, 1995.

Knight, P. & Story, K., *Spinning Heads*, Hawker Brownlow Education, Melbourne, 2001.

Locke, J., 'Reports with rapport', *Boys in schools bulletin*, vol. 3, no. 4.

Marsden, J., *Secret men's business*, Pan Macmillan, Sydney, 1998.

Martin, C., Arizona State University research published in *Journal of social and personal relationships* and reported in *The Sydney Morning Herald*, 21 May 2000.

McCalman, J., 'Why girls do better than boys in exams', *The Age*, 10 February 2000.

McCann, R., *On their own*, Finch, Sydney, 2000.

Moir, A. & Jessel D., *Brainsex*, Mandarin, London, 1989.

Moir, A. & B., *Why men don't iron*, Harper Collins, London, 1998.

Noonan, G., 'Boys take the honours – in wagging', *The Sydney Morning Herald*, 7 June 2001.

NSW Teachers Federation Centre for Teaching and Learning, 'Girls, boys and equity', NSW Teachers Federation, Sydney, 1994.

Olweus, D., *Aggression in schools: bullies and whipping boys*, Hemisphere, 1978.

Pease, A. & B., *Why men don't listen & women can't read maps*, Pease Training International, Sydney, 1998.

Parker, J., *Effective teaching and learning strategies for all students*, Hawker Brownlow Education, Melbourne, 1999.

Petersen, L., & Ganoni, A., 'Stop, think, do', Melbourne, ACER.

Phillips, G., & Gibbons, M., *27 Ways to improve classroom instruction*, Hawker Brownlow Education, Melbourne, 1996.

Pollack, W., *Real boys*, Scribe, Melbourne, 1999.

Rigby, K., 'Boys & bullying', *Boys in schools bulletin*, vol. 4, no. 4.

Rodda, R., 'Angry city', *The Daily Telegraph*, 3 July 2001.

Rogers, B., *Behaviour management*, Scholastic, Melbourne, 1995.

Rowe, Dr K., 'Exploding the "myths" and exploring "real" effects in the education of boys', *Boys in schools bulletin*, University of Newcastle, vol. 3, no. 3, 2000.

Rowe, Dr K., 'Equal and different? Yes, but what really matters?', background paper to keynote address presented to joint conference of The Alliance of Girls' Schools (Australasia) and The International Boys' Schools Coalition (Australian Hub) Southport School, Queensland, August 2001.

Shores, D., *Boys & Relationships*, University of Newcastle, 1999.

Slade, M., 'Listening to the boys' *Boys in schools journal*, vol. 4, no. 1.

Slade & Trent, 'What the boys are saying: examining the views of boys about declining rates of achievement and retention', *Boys in schools bulletin*, vol. 4 no. 1.

UHCMI & University of Newcastle, *Rural young men's health report*, Newcastle, 2000.

West, P., 'Boys underachievement in school: some persistent problems and some current research', *Issues in educational research*, vol. 9, no. 1, 1999.

Wood, M., 'Special schools for rowdy kids', *Herald Sun*, 17 June 2001.